97/83

ILLO
1

-3

GAYLORD MG

HADRIAN

Hadrian, a bust from his birthplace Italica (Santeponce), now in the Archaeological Museum at Seville.

HADRIAN

by

Stewart Perowne
M.A., F.S.A.

DORSET PRESS

New York

This edition published by Dorset Press
a division of Marboro Books Corporation,
by arrangement with Hodder and Stoughton Limited
1990 Dorset Press

ISBN 0-88029-469-8

Printed in the United States of America
10 9 8 7 6 5 4 3 2 1

TO

ROBIN MacGREGOR

SOURCES AND ACKNOWLEDGEMENTS

A. *Written Sources*

THESE are meagre, late and unsatisfactory. From Hadrian's autobiography, only six references have survived, embedded in the *Life* and Dio (see below). We have no literary source that can by any means be called contemporary. Such as they are, our chief ancient sources are two.

1. The *Life*, which is the first of thirty such Lives, covering the emperors, and their heirs, from Hadrian to Carinus and Numerian, that is the period from A.D. 117 to A.D. 284. The Lives are by various hands, some dedicated to Diocletian, some to Constantine, others to important Romans. The model which the writers of these Lives, generally known as the *Augustan History*, employed was Suetonius, a racy biographer of the second century, whose *Lives of the Twelve Caesars* gives a vivid and raffish account of the first century of the empire. He was at one time one of Hadrian's secretaries (see page 51). His imitators were by no means as able as he was, and suffered besides from the major defect that they wrote so long after the deaths of the men they set out to describe. The *Augustan History* is available in the Loeb edition, with an excellent introduction by Dr. David Magie of Princeton University, its translator.

2. The only other writer to deal at any length with Hadrian is Dio Cassius, a distinguished Bithynian who was twice consul, and published a history of Rome in eighty books about the year 200. Unfortunately, for the Life of Hadrian, which is contained in the sixty-ninth book, we are dependent on an epitome made in the eleventh century. This is not merely inadequate, but sometimes gives a completely wrong sense. The story of Favorinus (see page 105) is an example. In the *Lives of the Sophists*, by Philostratus, the anecdote is related as an example of Hadrian's *dégagé* wit: in the epitome, it is made to illustrate his arrogance. This may be intentional: the whole tenor of Dio is antagonistic to Hadrian. Dio was a senator, and Hadrian had, in his view, treated the senate badly. It is possible also that Hadrian's association with Antinoüs, who was also a Bithynian, and its tragic end, may have affected Dio's view. The epitome is referred to in this work as "the chronicler".

These two books, one of the fourth century, and one of the eleventh based on a work of the second century, are our only continuous sources. Certain minor writers give occasional help, such as Philostratus, already mentioned, and the fourth-century Sextus Aurelius Victor, whose *Caesars* is a very sketchy account of the emperors from Augustus to Constantius. It is from Victor, for example, that we learn how Hadrian came to plan his villa at Tibur. References to Hadrian— sometimes, in view of the general obscurity, illuminating—occur in the

7

writings of the fourth-century Christian authors Epiphanius, Eusebius and Jerome, and in those of Orosius, who wrote in the fifth century.

B. *Papyri, Inscriptions and Coins* are most important sources of information. The number of the two former is constantly being added to, and unrecorded coins still turn up.

C. Modern Writers

The standard work in Englishon the emperor Hadrian is, and is likely to remain, *The Life and Principate of the Emperor Hadrian A.D. 76–138*, by Bernard W. Henderson, which was first published in 1923. It is the work of a scholar, who had devoted fifteen years to its composition. The chapter in the *Cambridge Ancient History*, Volume XI, by Wilhelm Weber, is not regarded as among that great historian's greatest achievements. It is unprecise and sentimental. *Magnificent Hadrian*, by Sulamith Ish Kishor, London, 1935, is a spritely, humorous and sympathetic study of Hadrian's character. "Mme Yourcenar"'s *Mémoires d'Hadrien*, which first appeared in Paris in 1952, and is now available in an English translation supervised by the author herself, is internationally famous. It is one of the most scholarly and beautiful psychological romances of our age. The latest objective work on Hadrian and certainly one of the best, is *L'Empereur Hadrien: Oeuvre Législative et Administrative* by Bernard d'Orgeval, Paris, 1950. It is a book for students, and is very learned. For the work of Hadrian in Asia, David Magie's *Roman Rule in Asia Minor*, Princeton, 1950, is invaluable. For his dealings with the Levant, Abel's *Histoire de la Palestine depuis la conquête d'Alexandre jusqu'à l'invasion arabe* is the best guide. The Jewish question is very ably dealt with in the *Prolegomena to the Corpus Papyrorum Judaicarum* Volume I, Harvard, 1957, by the late Victor Tcherikover.

Naturally, in preparing a study of this sort, I have had constant recourse to many other works, some being standard histories, encyclopaedias and dictionaries, such as may be found in every major library, others articles in specialist periodicals, to which I have been directed by kind friends. It would be tedious to enumerate them all; but the article on *Religion and Literature in Hadrian's Policy*, by W. den Boer, in *Mnemosyne*, S. iv. Vol. VIII,[2] 1955, Lloyd William Daly's contribution on the *sententiae* to the *Illinois Studies in Language and Literature*, 1939, and Marta Sordi's *I primi rapporti fra lo Stato romano e il Cristianesimo*, in the Rendiconti morali of the Accademia dei Lincei, 1957, Serie VIII, Vol. XII, fasc. 1 and 2 are worthy of special mention.

One particular difficulty besets the writer on Hadrian, and that is the itineraries and dating of his journeys. On this subject two things may be said: first, no two modern authorities agree on the routes and dates. Some scholars even deny that Hadrian ever visited towns which others are sure he did; secondly, at this distance of time, it is not of the first importance to know, within a year or so, just when Hadrian was in such and such a city, provided that we have the general outline of his journeys and the general impact of his policy correct; and that we have.

The following works are named only because a reader who wishes to learn more about the period will find them of great help:

Roman Imperial Civilisation, by Harold Mattingly, 1957.

The Handbook to the Roman Wall, by the late J. Collingwood Bruce, current edition.

Roman Britain, by I. A. Richmond, 1955, being the first volume of the Pelican History of England.

Daily Life in Ancient Rome, by Jérôme Carcopino, now available in a Penguin edition, translated by E. O. Lorimer, with Professor Henry T. Rowell's notes.

Les Réligions paganes dans l'Empire Romaine, by Franz Cumont, 1928 edn.

A New Eusebius, documents illustrative of the history of the Church to A.D. 337, edited by J. Stevenson, 1957.

Das Romische Herscherbild (Deutches Archäologisches Institut) Hadrian, Plotina, Marciana, Matidia, Sabina, von Max Wegner, Berlin, 1956.

Stadte Pamphyliens und Pisidiens, K. Lanckoronski, Vienna, 1890.

Gli Obelischi Egiziani di Roma, Orazio Marucchi, Rome, 1898.

Scavi di Ostia, Libreria dello Stato, Rome, 1953.

For the monuments in Rome and Italy, the *Libretti Azzuri*, the official guides issued by the *Direzione Generale Della Antichita E Belle Arti* of the *Ministero Della Pubblica Istruzzione* are models of their kind. Dr. Roberto Vighi's monograph on the Pantheon is invaluable.

Of those who have helped me the list is long. The Master and Fellows of Corpus Christi College once again allowed me to reside in College during the Long Vacation of 1958, and so to get the book started. The Director and Staff of the British School at Rome did all in their power to forward my researches, and so did Dr. Roberto Vighi himself. For information on various aspects of the subject I have to thank M. Seyrig, Director of the Institut Français d'Archéologie in Beirut, Professor Norman Bentwich and Dr. S. Applebaum of the Hebrew University, Mr. R. D. Barnett and Mr. D. J. Wiseman of the British Museum, Professor C. H. O. Scaife and Dr. D. Baramki, both of the American University of Beirut, Señor Juan de M. Carrizao, Director of the Excavations at Italica, Señor Juan Lafita Y Diaz, Director of the Seville Archaeological Museum, and Father Joseph Crehan, S. J. Mr. Geoffrey Woodhead, Classical Praelector of Corpus Christi College, Cambridge, has again given me the benefit of his scholarship and has again read the typescript.

Finally, and very specially, I thank Sir Hugh and Lady Foot, in whose beautiful Cyprus home the greater part of this book was written.

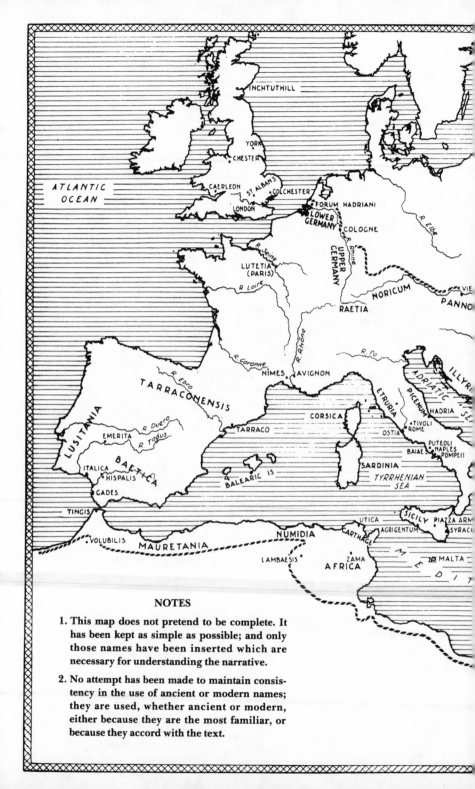

NOTES

1. This map does not pretend to be complete. It has been kept as simple as possible; and only those names have been inserted which are necessary for understanding the narrative.

2. No attempt has been made to maintain consistency in the use of ancient or modern names; they are used, whether ancient or modern, either because they are the most familiar, or because they accord with the text.

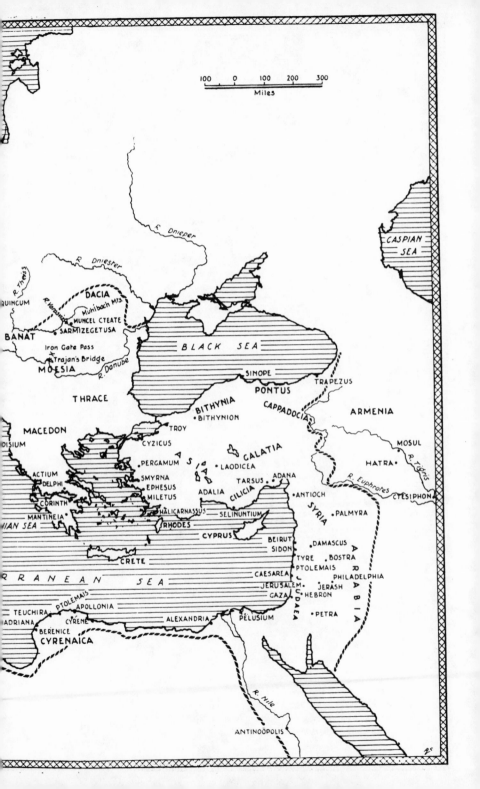

CONTENTS

LIST OF ILLUSTRATIONS

Key to Acknowledgements

[1] Museo Arqueologico Provincial, Sevilla.

[2] Corpus Christi College, Cambridge.

[3] Museo di Ostia.

[4] Professor Michael Grant and *The Geographical Magazine*.

[5] Alinari.

[6] Archivio Fotografico Gall. Mus. Vaticani.

[7] Trustees of the Chatsworth Settlement, by permission of the Librarian, Chatsworth.

[8] Ministry of Works, Crown Copyright reserved.

[9] From a drawing by A. Terenzio (phot. Soprint. Monumenti del Lazio).

[10] Archivio Fotografico, Ufficio Centrale, Mon. Mus. e Gall. Pontif.

[11] Rev. David Brewster.

[12] Aubrey Halford Esq.

[13] Dames de Zion.

[14] Rex Studios.

[15] Anderson.

[16] Bibliothèque Nationale.

[17] Museo Nazionale, Palestrina.

[18] Ny Carlsberg Glyptothek.

[19] Louvre.

INTRODUCTION

DURING the years 1956 to 1958 I undertook a study of the dynasty of the Herods of Judaea, which resulted in two books, *The Life and Times of Herod the Great* and *The Later Herods*, both of which were published by Messrs Hodder & Stoughton. The period covered by these essays was one of the most formative in history, being that during which both the Roman Empire and Christianity came into existence. To an investigation of that period, a consideration of the emperor Hadrian is a natural sequel, first because the principate of the emperor Hadrian is generally agreed to have marked the zenith of the Roman Empire as a political and social institution, and secondly because it was Hadrian who made the triumph of Christianity inevitable. He did not intend this result; but by elevating a young favourite into godhead he reduced polytheism to absurdity, and so turned men's minds increasingly to monotheism. By obliterating Jerusalem of the Jews, he ensured that when monotheism prevailed it would prevail in its Christian form.

Thus it was that I was led to contemplate a study of Hadrian. But even without the foregoing reasons, which seem weighty enough, there are two others which attract a twentieth-century student to this bygone emperor. The first reason for Hadrian's contemporary appeal is this. In the middle of the twentieth century, we find ourselves at one of the great turning-points of history. Just as in the second millennium before Christ Stone-age man found himself confronted by a new age founded on metals, first bronze and then iron, so now metallic man must come to terms with a new, nuclear age. Instinctively, as the vast horizon displays itself, in order to brace ourselves for the unknown, we cling to the known. In order to face the future, we turn to the past, to its security, its certainty, its peace. Of the world as we still know it, Hadrian was one of the principal architects. The second reason is Hadrian himself. He was a man of great versatility and achievement: soldier, statesman and humanist, a political innovator whose views more than any other Roman emperor find a response in our own contemporary ideals. Yet, though Hadrian

15

seems so close to our own age and spirit, he eludes us. He is still, as he was to the Romans of his day, an enigma; and an enigma, an unsolved mystery, always attracts.

My object in the present study is to discuss Hadrian as a political and religious philosopher and as an artist, because I believe that it is these aspects of the man that make the strongest appeal today. Even for that limited task I have few qualifications. The chief of them is fortuitous. Hadrian was a great traveller: he visited nearly every province of the empire. It happens that it has been my lot to visit many of the same places myself, and so to acquire, over a period of years, an enthusiasm for Hadrian which is all that I can offer in place of scholarship.

S. P.

Chapter I

THE ETERNAL CITY

ROME in the year A.D. 86 was an unhappy city. Once again, the Great Experiment had failed. One hundred and sixteen years earlier, Romans reflected, a century of domestic turmoil, rivalry and bloodshed had been ended by the adoption of a novel form of government. The old so-called republic, the city-democracy which had made Rome great, and the Mediterranean Sea a Roman lake, this austere and majestic polity, was melted down, and recast as an empire, the rule of one man. Not that it was called an empire. No names had been changed: the fiction of the republic was maintained. But it was one sole man, Caesar, who ruled now, and to him must be rendered the things that were his. The first imperial "Caesar" was Caius Julius Caesar Octavianus Augustus, the great-nephew and heir of the famous Julius Caesar, whose assassination in 44 B.C. had precipitated the final round in the dynastic contest which was to decide the future of Rome for centuries to come. When, in the year 31, Octavian defeated the combined hosts of Mark Antony and Cleopatra, the world was his. Rome was grateful to him. He had given them peace at home and glory abroad. He gave them wealth and, above all, the prospect of stability, which within the memory of living man no Roman had known. In return, the Romans were quite content that this one man should rule. They called him *princeps*, first citizen, *augustus*, worshipful, and it is as Augustus that he has ever since been known. For more than forty years, this cold but capable man ruled the Roman world. Helped by a minister of outstanding genius, Marcus Vipsanius Agrippa, Augustus overhauled the administration, both domestic and provincial, and bequeathed to his countrymen one of the greatest political creations of all time, the Roman Empire.

For almost a century his fabric endured unimpaired. The principate was not, in theory, hereditary, but in a rather make-shift manner it did, in fact, become so. Augustus was succeeded by a stepson, Tiberius (the Caesar of the Gospels), Tiberius by a

17

great-nephew, Caligula, Caligula by an uncle, Claudius. Not all these men had been good men, but the machine had worked and the citizens had been secure. Then came Nero, Claudius' great-nephew and stepson, and with him came disaster. In the year 68, Rome had been revisited by the fire and steel of civil war. Now, only eighteen years later, the Romans were once again trembling "lest intermitted vengeance arm again his red right hand to plague us". To form some idea of the disquiet which harrowed the minds of Romans in the year A.D. 86, it would be necessary for an Englishman to imagine that in the year 1805, when England was about to embark on the most arduous and splendid period of her history, the subjects of King George III were beginning to suspect that the settlement of 1688 had been a delusive failure.

What had produced this malaise? The civil war which followed the death of Nero, who had escaped assassination only by suicide, had thrown up four "emperors" in a single year, of whom the last, Vespasian, became the final winner. He was of obscure origin, but he had proved himself a capable general, first in Britain and then in Palestine; and it was the confidence of the army that led to his elevation as emperor. After the vicious eccentricities of the later Julio-Claudians, as the rulers from Augustus to Nero are known, and after the ruin of civil war, Rome was glad enough to be ruled for nine years by this dull but reliable man. He had already had his two sons, Titus and Domitian, proclaimed "Caesar" by the pliant senate, thereby ensuring that each in his turn should be master of Rome. This was a new departure: a step towards the open and general recognition of the hereditary principle which had hitherto been only tacitly and retrospectively accepted in each particular case.

But heredity was by no means yet the sole and secure basis for succession. At Nero's death, says Tacitus in a famous phrase, "the great secret was divulged that emperors could be made elsewhere than in Rome", that is to say by the army. Henceforth, no emperor could rule unchallenged unless the army was prepared to accept him. Vespasian was a soldier, and it thus came about that senate, people and army were all willing to see him found a dynasty, if he could, because, as many a nation has discovered since, the most frequent alternative to the hereditary system is the chaos of successive *coups d'état*; and thus it comes about that a people will support one or more ineffective or reprobate rulers rather than be afflicted by the continual uncertainty of competitive power. The new dynasty started off well. Titus, athletic and affable, delighted the Romans, who called him "the world's darling". Unfortunately he reigned for only two years, during which, with a campaign in Britain to supervise, the destruction of Pompeii and Herculaneum to cope with, and the ravages of a fire in the capital to repair, he had little time for the arts of peace. He was only forty-two when he died, to be succeeded by his younger brother, a sad contrast to the amiable Titus. He was a cruel lout, who displayed all the arrogance that only humble birth can bestow. He hated the old aristocracy, and he hated the people as well. He could not forget that as a boy he had escaped the fury of a Roman mob only by the humiliating shift of disguising himself as a priest of Isis. He scowled at writers, whom he suspected of being "subversive", and at philosophers, who were notoriously "seditious". He set up a police state. Under a cloak of hypocritical puritanism, he affected to punish vice, rigorously enforcing the laws against incest and sodomy, to both of which he was himself addicted. He pretended to encourage Italian agriculture by the ridiculous and unenforceable expedient of forbidding viticulture in the provinces. He simulated humanity, proscribing the castration of males, and even setting a controlled price on eunuchs to mitigate the shortage which he knew must ensue. But soon he showed his true colours. No one was safe. His favourite pastime was spearing flies, but his fellow-creatures quickly discovered that absence and silence were the master virtues of the age. His religious views were as strict as they were simple: he, Domitian, was both god and lord, and to be addressed as such. He loathed the Jews, and the Christians as well.

The Rome of Domitian possessed neither spiritual energy nor artistic vigour with which to offset and overcome the deficiencies of its ruler. It was neither splendid nor cultivated. Because we know ancient Rome either from "reconstructions", diffused with perpetual sunshine for ever reflected from temples and palaces of unblemished marble, or from the aspect of the Forum and Palatine as it now is, we are apt to think that it was always the finished wonder of the antique world, perfect, timeless and imperishable: the Eternal City, as its sons were beginning to call it in the days of Vespasian. The truth is far different. The majority of the citizens lived in blocks of squalid, multi-storeyed flats crowded together in unhealthy slums, liable alike to flood and fire. Moreover, not only was Rome vulnerable to the changes that assault any city, but within the last twenty-two years it had thrice been ravaged by calamity. First there was the famous fire of Nero's reign, in 64, when more of the city had been destroyed, proportionately, than was gutted in the great fire of London in 1666. Two-thirds of Rome, including the Palatine hill, had been obliterated. Five years later, in the tumults that marked the "year of the four emperors", the Capitol, the Downing Street of Rome, had been burnt, and the whole of the record office destroyed. To crown the city's misfortune, another fire in A.D. 80 had wiped out a great part of it, including the Pantheon, several other temples and some important libraries. By no means all of this damage had been repaired by the year 86. But the most arresting landmark in the whole of ancient Rome was a new building which had escaped the fire, namely the Colosseum, or to give it its proper name the Flavian amphitheatre, after the patronymic of Vespasian and Titus who had built it on the site of part of Nero's Golden House; Titus had inaugurated it in the year 80. There it stood, new and glistening (though its top storey was of wood when it was first built). It was the pride of Rome, whose ruler engraved it on his coins (see Plate 1), so that its fame might spread throughout the empire.

The name Rome is today associated reflexively, inevitably, with the great shrine which dominates it, St. Peter's, and with the faith of which it is the centre. The name and the faith are one. In a similar way, and to the same degree, the Colosseum dominated and expressed ancient Rome. In this contrast of the two buildings is summed up and epitomised the contrast between the outlook and aspiration of an ancient Roman and a modern Christian. The Colosseum was a temple of slaughter, a great rotunda dedicated to the destruction of human and animal life, in which fifty thousand citizens could witness and applaud the shedding of human blood. It is easy to be hypocritical about the spectacles of the amphitheatre. Even Christian saints have left us descriptions of the horrible fascination which the contests of the gladiators held for them, once they had entered the theatre; and the modern bullfight, in its setting, its solemnity, and the thrill of its perils and dangers, is the direct descendant in unbroken line of the Roman amphitheatre and the Roman spectacle. Nevertheless, the callous brutality of the Colosseum, its erection into a cult, respectable and invigorating, is the supreme expression of the coarseness which from first to last disfigured the Roman character.

Such was the Rome, the Eternal City, to which, in the year 86 came a boy from Spain. His name was Hadrian, and he was one day to be its ruler.

Chapter II

THE YOUNG SPANIARD

HADRIAN, the future Roman emperor, was born at Italica, in southern Spain, on 24th January, A.D. 76. His full name was Publius Aelius Hadrianus, the same as that of his father. The first name, Publius, was personal. Aelius was the family name, or surname, as we call it. Romans often added a third name. Sometimes this was a nickname, as for instance Cicero, the most famous of all, which means a chick-pea. In Hadrian's case the third name was like those descriptions which the Scots so conveniently add to a name—"of so-and-so". It meant "Of Hadria", that is, sprung from the town of Hadria in Picenum, the district on the north-east coast of Italy which fronts the Adriatic or Hadriatic sea. It was from there that his forebears had come nearly three centuries before.

When, in 205 B.C., the great Scipio Africanus had driven the Carthaginians from Spain, he decided to try the experiment of planting communities of veteran Roman soldiers on Spanish soil. The plan was to prove as successful as the later planting of European colonies on American soil. Among these groups was one which was granted land in the fertile south. It was made up of sick and wounded men. Their travelling days were over, and so, to commemorate the motherland they would not see again, they called their little town Italica, the Italian. These veterans married women of the country, that is of native Iberian, Phoenician or even Greek stock, for all of these strains were to be found in Spain at the time of the Roman conquest; and archaeological findings shew that they co-existed with the newcomers. Later waves of colonisation founded new cities. In the days of Augustus, for instance, some veterans were established at a settlement they called Emerita, now Merida. But the Hadrians were proud of being among the "First Families" of the province, descended from the original settlers.

Not that they considered themselves provincial. They would have repudiated that slight. For one thing, Spain was the richest single possession of Rome. It produced gold and silver and lead and tin. Its olive oil was better than that of Italy. For another, in the century which saw Hadrian's birth, it nourished a literary school that had practically dominated Roman literature. Seneca, Lucan, Quintilian, Martial and a host of lesser writers all sprang from Spain. And Italica was situated in the most beautiful region of the whole peninsula, in Baetica, that is the rich plain in the far south athwart the lower reaches of the Guadalquivir, the *Wadi al Kebir* or Great River, for so the Arabs called it when they in their turn colonised Spain. In Roman days the river was called Baetis, and the region Baetica. It formed a small province by itself, administered by the Roman senate through a proconsul, who needed no troops to help him keep order. The rest of the country was divided between Lusitania, roughly modern Portugal, and Tarraconensis, which comprised the remainder of the peninsula. From the Arabs we have taken their name for Baetica, Andalusia (originally Vandalusia, after the Vandals whom the Arabs dispossessed). The word suggests all that is fair and pleasant. Still, as of old, it is a paradise; and it is not hard to understand why, in that luxuriant climate, even the rigours of Islam, the severity of its architecture and decoration, were to become gentle and almost lush.

The most southerly part of continental Europe, Andalusia lies on about the same latitude as Sicily. The Roman veterans must have been delighted with such a country, just as the English colonists of Virginia were to be, and for the same reason. It was possible to construct in Baetica an Italian life, but on a far grander scale.

Nowhere in Italy, not even in the valley of the Po, are there such vast, rolling plains, such fertile, undulating downs, as adorn Andalusia. The country bears a superficial resemblance to the motherland (as it was then) of Italy. But every amenity is here to be found in a heightened degree. The verdure is richer, the rivers wider, the soil deeper, the distances greater. The chief town of the region was called Hispalis, a native Iberian name, now known to us, through the Arab *Ishbiliya*, as Seville. It was both the capital of the province and a port, as it still is. Italica, too, was an important town, as it has long ceased to be.

Five miles to the west of modern Seville there lies a little village called Santeponce. It bestrides two rounded hillocks, about half a mile south of the Guadalquivir, towards which they slope. From this gentle eminence, away to the right as one faces north, the spires and towers of Seville spangle the horizon. In front, the great plain of Andalusia, veined by the river, sweeps up to the Sierra Morena. It is as fair a countryside as Europe has to shew. On the little hills at our feet are the remains of a Roman town, Italica. It is built, we notice, on the usual Roman plan, four-square, with the main street, the *cardo maximus* or *chief hinge* as they called it, running north and south, as it habitually did. This alignment assured that houses on both sides of the principal artery would get their fair share of both morning and evening sun. We can see at once that this is no mere village: it is a fine large town. Not much of it has been excavated as yet; but already we can see that it, like the average town in Roman Britain, covered a hundred and thirty acres; that is as much as St. James' and Mayfair put together. The main street is two kilometres long and sixteen metres, more than fifty feet, wide, the widest, it is said, in the whole empire. The cross streets are three-quarters that width. Every one of them was shaded with porticoes on both sides. The piers are made of the finest brickwork, in a cruciform pattern that we generally associate with the Renaissance. Splendid houses flanked the roads, with fine pavements, baths and courts. There were two public baths as well, a theatre, hotel and gymnasium. These buildings, to judge from the remnants of them which are all that we now see, were much finer than those of Pompeii. Beneath the great main street ran the town sewer. At the end of it, as it slopes down towards the north, we see the ruined bulk of a huge amphitheatre. We are not surprised to learn that it was the fourth largest in the whole empire, being surpassed only by those of Pola and Pozzuoli, and the great Colosseum of Rome itself.

The grandeur of Italica, as it remains to us now, is undoubtedly due to the pious embellishment of the city in the days of the Antonines, that is of the emperors who followed Hadrian, when the town could boast of having given Rome two emperors in succession, for Trajan, Hadrian's predecessor and cousin, was also born at Italica; but the plan as we see it now is the plan of the town with which Hadrian was familiar as a child. Hadrian's father was the son of a lady called Ulpia, the sister of Marcus Ulpius Trajanus, senior, a distinguished soldier, who, ten years

24

before Hadrian's birth, had commanded a division during Vespasian's victorious campaign in Judaea. He later became consul and then governor of Asia. His son, Marcus Ulpius Trajanus, junior, became emperor in the year 98 (see Tables I and II). Thus, Hadrian was born a first cousin once removed of a future emperor, of a man who by birth was "in the running" for the highest office. His father, too, was a man of distinction. He may well have won the name *Afer*, the African, for service in Mauretania. He had been a praetor, that is the judicial magistrate inferior only to the consuls and of senatorial rank. To the boy from Italica, such heredity and such connexions were bound to be a presage of eminence. Hadrian's mother was called Domitia Paulina, good old Roman names, though she herself came from Cadiz, the gateway of the Atlantic, the port on the seaway that led to Ireland and to Britain. Hadrian's mother may well have had Iberian, or even Irish blood in her veins. Between Ireland and Spain there were ancient ties, which have lasted down to our own day, when the Spanish flag is conspicuous on the trawlers that visit Bantry Bay every summer.

By heredity, therefore, young Hadrian was endowed with a wide range of interest. His upbringing was to increase it. First and foremost, in the Italica of his day Hadrian would feel himself to be a true Roman, in the great Roman tradition. His youthful gaze would fall upon statues of Alexander, of the great Augustus, and on other works of art, which, to judge from those which are preserved in the Seville Museum, were of a very high quality, not at all the sort of mediocre stuff which might be expected to adorn a provincial city. It is far more "Roman" for example than that which has been recovered from Merida. Secondly, just across the river was Ilipa, now Alcala del Fin, the site of the battle which had given Spain to Rome. From it, the young Roman must have acquired a pride in being Roman, such as an Englishman gains from the contemplation of Gibraltar. Thirdly, there were the mosaics in the houses. These are of great interest. Many of them display the usual classical subjects, Medusa, Flora, Bacchus, Silenus and the rest. But there is another class, which stresses an alien theme, namely Africa. One floor, for instance, bears a representation, common enough, of a number of different birds. This subject always tempted the virtuosity of the mosaicist, because the aim was to represent the soft delicacy of feathers through the medium of *tesserae* of hard stone. It is natural to find such a mosaic in one of the big houses of Italica. But, in this case, all the birds have been identified as birds of Africa. After all, Africa was only just across the straits, only a hundred miles from the town itself. There is another composition which shews Africa in a different light. It is rather crude, in black-and-white, probably the work of a local artist. It represents a burlesque of African Negroes, in humiliating and indecent postures, locked in strife with overpowering monsters. With Africa the citizens of Italica might have dealings, but Africa was alien, "native", inferior and hostile. Young Hadrian would receive a view of "foreigners" and their ideas that would imbue him with a lack of sympathy for un-Roman or un-Greek people and ideas. During his adult life, he was often to shew it. Here we may find the origin of this trait, akin to the irrational antipathy sometimes felt by modern "whites" who grow up in proximity with people of another race.

Hadrian was endowed with a fine physique. He was tall, well made and very strong. He had curly hair, which he kept carefully combed. He was an ardent athlete, and loved hunting. What runs he must have enjoyed over the plain, and up in the sierra, where the boar and stag still abound. But he had a mind to match his body. His was a remarkably gifted personality—"the universal genius" in the words of H. A. L. Fisher. He loved the classics, so much so that he was called the Greekling by his contemporaries. He sang, wrote poetry, was a painter and sculptor, too. As an architect he was to win abiding renown. Looking at the sensitive, thoughtful face that his busts reveal to us (see Frontispiece), we feel that we have in Hadrian a character of the Cinquecento, rather than "an antique Roman". Roman he was, by birth and upbringing, but Greek by the inclination of his nature. His life was to shew him in both guises, and sometimes he was to be torn between the two. He could be firm, industrious, calm and just. He could be inventive, sensitive, an innovator and an artist. When his psychological balance was upset, by opposition, or by attraction, he was to prove callous and even cruel, or lascivious and vain.

When Hadrian was ten, his father died. Of his mother we know nothing. Even if she were still alive, male guardians would be necessary. Young Hadrian was naturally committed to the most influential available, which meant his cousin Trajan, and a fellow-townsman called Acilius Attianus. If these two were the choice of Hadrian's mother, then she was a most far-seeing parent. Trajan had been a praetor the year before. He was then appointed to command one of the two legions in Spain and so may have been in the country when his cousin died. The other guardian, Attianus, was an *eques* or knight, that is a member of the secondary élite, who were now coming more and more to the fore in administration. Certain key posts were reserved for knights, and one of these, sure enough, Attianus was to hold at a critical juncture in Hadrian's fortunes. Trajan was soon called away for service on the northern frontier of the empire, that is on the Rhine. The care of Hadrian and responsibility for his education devolved on Attianus. He took the boy off to Rome, and there he stayed for the next five years.

It is not to be wondered at that the boy from Italica found little to admire and emulate there. This child of the Andalusian plain, the athlete and huntsman of the sierra, bred in the bracing simplicity of a remote and decent province, could not be expected to find himself at home in Domitian's capital. To the end of his days, Hadrian and Rome never came to terms with each other. On the boy from Italica the great mother city made such an unfavourable impression that he decided that it might well be an advantage for a Roman not to be born in Rome, that the provinces were to be regarded just as highly as Italy, that the capital, venerable and august as it was, was by no means synonymous with the empire, and that society, if the life of the ordinary citizens was to be secure and happy, required a direction such as neither the accepted moral and religious standards nor a Domitian could give it. As to where that direction was to come from and how it was to be applied, Hadrian's whole life would be spent finding out. As he returned to Italica, the young Greekling, at the age of fifteen, thought he knew where to look for it.

Chapter III

TOWARDS THE SUN

BACK in Italica, it is to be presumed that Hadrian lived once more with his family, but of this we have no knowledge. What we do know is that the object of his being sent back to Spain by Attianus was to toughen him up. His guardian rightly thought that a longer sojourn in Rome would make this young intellectual too narrow, too bookish, and that what he needed was some open air. Perhaps, too, Hadrian had already given evidence of that overbearing pride, amounting to vanity, and of the jealousy which was the unfortunate foil of his splendid talents. At all events, we are told that he "immediately entered on military service", a baffling phrase. There were no legions in peaceful Baetica, and military service must have been a mere form of speech. What Hadrian actually spent his time on was hunting. Those plains and mountains, how stimulating to see them again at his door, after the crowded life of the Roman Forum. Hadrian, it is pleasant to record, gave himself passionately to the chase, an occupation which is a natural tonic for both mind and body. By a kindly irony, it was Hadrian's obsession with hunting that brought him into the main stream of history. His brother-in-law, Servianus, thirty-one years older than Hadrian, was jealous of the brilliant and charming boy. (Perhaps Hadrian's mother was now dead, and he living with his married sister.) He sought to discredit him with his guardian Trajan. Trajan was now a man of note. He was not yet forty, but he was a general with an established reputation, and he had already served his year as consul. Above all, he was in favour with Domitian, by whom he had stood at a very dangerous crisis, only two years before, when a general on the Rhine, called Saturninus, had revolted against Domitian and had nearly rekindled civil war. Trajan had shewn his loyalty by a forced march which brought him to Domitian's side. The danger had, in fact, been overcome before Trajan arrived, but Domitian was grateful to him in his fashion. Servianus now wrote to Trajan, saying that Hadrian did nothing but

Nerva (page 32).

The Colosseum as originally constructed, with wooden top storey and poles for the awnings (page 20).

Domitian (page 18).

The main street of Italica, with Seville in the background.

The amphitheatre at Italica (page 24).

hunt, and that he was extravagant and had run into debt. Trajan's reply was to summon the boy to Rome. So, after only two years away from the capital, Hadrian returned to it, and into the very highest circle of its society.

Trajan was charmed by his young cousin. His book-learning did not irritate the soldier, who indeed, like many men of action, sought the society of scholars and was liked by them in return. Nevertheless, it must have been the virile young athlete, handsome and tough, who captivated Trajan. We know little of Trajan, except from the testimony of his famous column, which in historical narrative still expounds to us his virtues and victories; as Gibbon put it we are dependent for what we do know on "the glimmerings of an abridgment, or the doubtful light of a panegyric". Dio Cassius records that "he drank all the wine he wanted, and in his relations with boys he harmed no one", for in the Roman society of the day, vice was accounted as no more than an eccentricity, even if as much. It was no doubt a physical attraction that drew Trajan to his ward. Trajan "treated him like a son", and this, we are told, aroused the resentment of the guardians of "certain boys whom Trajan loved ardently".

Education in Rome was just beginning to be formalised when Hadrian had first gone there. It was a Spaniard, Quintilian, who opened the first regular college and became the first instructor to receive a regular salary from the state. He has left us a treatise on education as he thought it should be conducted. The whole work is of interest, both for its theory—which anticipates so much that we regard as recent psychological discovery—and for its literary criticism. He was a favourite of Domitian, whose nephew he taught, and it is more than likely that Hadrian also was among his pupils. From our point of view, and with regard to Hadrian's future cultural outlook, one of Quintilian's most pertinent principles is that concerning language. The ordinary educated Roman had for several generations been fluent in both Latin and Greek, just as a modern Scandinavian of comparable status will know his own language and English as well. The two tongues were referred to simply as "both languages"—it was unnecessary to specify which they were. Horace, a century before, wishing to flatter his patron Maecenas, calls him "master of both languages". And so the cult of bilingualism had continued, until Quintilian, at the very outset of his book, found it necessary to tell parents which of the two a child should learn first. He comes down on the side of Greek, on the ground that a boy will pick up Latin anyway, but warns against the intrusion of Hellenisms into the vernacular. His fellow Spaniard Hadrian certainly followed his rule.

The Romans were a practical race: education must result in doing something. So young Hadrian, the hunter and Hellenist. must now be introduced into official life. Trajan found him a job. The Roman official hierarchy had originally been carefully graded, office by office, and age by age, so as to ensure as far as possible that only the best men should rise to the top and that by the time they did so they should be mature and experienced. The highest rank was that of consul, to which under the republic no one might attain before the age of forty. Under the empire, the regulations were progressively relaxed, so that mere children might be nominated consuls; nor was the office necessarily annual, as it had originally been. Three or four months would now reckon as a "consulate", after which the holder would be eligible for a first-class governorship. For a lad like Hadrian, the entry to the profession was still through a minor magistracy. There were six of these, and the one to which Hadrian was appointed was in the Probate court, a position of responsibility which would bring him into personal contact with many of the prominent people of Rome. Hadrian also held two other minor posts, in connexion with the organisation of ceremonials and the keeping of the official calendar. The Roman system drew no hard and fast line between civil and military command, just as in the British system, to this day, the civil governor of a colony is still the commander-in-chief as well, and many of the most successful governors are drawn from the higher ranks of the army. In the Roman Empire this duality began at the bottom of the scale. So it was that Hadrian was soon posted as a tribune, or company officer, of the IInd Legion, *Adjutrix*, as it was called, or *Auxiliary*, for Roman Legions, like British regiments, had nicknames as well as numbers. The IInd was called Auxiliary, because Vespasian had raised it from an auxiliary force of marines. The regiment had been serving at Chester, but had recently been transferred by Domitian to Buda-Pesth, then called Aquincum.

Thus Hadrian was introduced to the northern frontier of the empire. Down to our own age, the city of Buda-Pesth has preserved its quality of the last guardian of the West, the ultimate outpost of the Latin world. So it must have impressed young Hadrian. Behind him, as he looked out over the waters of the Danube, lay the province of Pannonia, as it was called, wrapped in what Pliny had lauded as "the immeasurable majesty of the Roman peace". To the south, to the east and to the west, province after province breathed the same air of tranquillity, warmed by the same radiance, nourished by the same security. The boundary and bulwark of this happy world had been formed, it seemed by nature herself, in the two great rivers, the Rhine and the Danube. Beyond the wide stream which at Buda-Pesth runs almost north and south lay the great plain of Hungary, across which swept hordes of savage and greedy men, sometimes as fawning traders, sometimes as ruthless assailants. Unknown, untrusted and un-tamed, these restless neighbours demanded that year in year out, by day and night, in summer and in winter, the Roman legions should stand alert upon the banks of the two rivers, for it was here that the Roman peace, the life of Rome itself, was guarded and preserved. On Hadrian, the situation, the contrast which it displayed, the lesson which it taught must have made a deep and lasting impression. He was to visit other frontiers of Rome, in the Levant, in Africa and in England; but always it would be this first experience of the *limes*, the *limit* of Roman authority, which he would remember. It was to be thorough, because in the following year, 96, when Hadrian was twenty, he was transferred to the Vth, the Macedonian, which was holding the province of Lower Moesia, that is the northern part of Bulgaria which fronts the Black Sea south of the Danube.

In that same year Domitian was assassinated. Like Nero, whom he resembled in his pride and lechery, he well knew the hazards of his position, and tried to guard against them in the same way, by murder. Seneca once said to Nero, "Remember, how ever many men you may kill, you can't kill your successor". Domitian described the same quandary of the tyrant, when he remarked that the lot of a prince was utterly wretched, because when he discovered a plot against his life nobody believed him unless he were dead. Domitian, like Nero, died a tyrant's death. The choice of a successor therefore lay with the senate. Domitian had left no natural heir, nor had he adopted one; he was only forty-four. The position of the senate under the empire resembled in some way that of the College of Cardinals under the modern

31

papacy, in that while it has little corporate power in normal times, to belong to it is a coveted honour, and, when a Pope dies, it is the College which elects a successor. So the senate, which normally was obsequious to the point of impotence, on the death of an emperor corporately appointed a new one. On this occasion it chose a feeble but honest old gentleman called Nerva. He was sixty-five. Nerva reversed all Domitian's oppressive decrees. The exiles were restored, Domitian's gold and silver images were melted down, prisoners on trial for treason were released, the informers were executed and the persecution of the Jews and Christians, and of those who adhered to them, was stopped. In fact, some people thought that Nerva went too far, and one of the consuls remarked that it had been bad enough to have an emperor who allowed no one to do anything, but it was even worse to have one who allowed everyone to do everything. Nevertheless, in general Nerva's reign was welcomed for its clemency.

Nerva had no children, and was not expected to live long. It was important that he should nominate his heir, indeed he was forced to do so by the threat of a military insurrection. Therefore, towards the end of the year 97, he formally ascended the Capitol to announce his choice. Whom would he choose? One of his own relations? He had many. Or a prominent Roman? Or a provincial—one of Italian stock like Vespasian, or even one of those intelligent southerners of Greek descent? Everyone was agog, when Nerva in a loud voice proclaimed: "May good fortune bless the Roman senate and people and myself. I, Marcus Nerva, hereby adopt as my son Marcus Ulpius Nerva Trajan"—adding his own name of Nerva, to those of Trajan, to seal the fact.

The Roman senate and people were surprised indeed, but content. Trajan had been sent north again, to the frontier, to Upper Germany this time, as governor, and he had just sent back to the senate a despatch announcing a victory. He was a sound, successful servant of Rome, only forty-four. He was the first "foreigner", the first man from outside Italy, ever to be nominated as emperor; but loyalty and ability were of more importance than birth.

Hadrian, who was now also in Germany, had reason to be content, too. Years ago, his old great-uncle Aelius, an acknowledged expert in prediction, had foretold that young Hadrian would bear rule one day. Just lately, when he had been in

Trajan. A coin in the British Museum, on which among his titles occur "German" and "Dacian", to commemorate his victories in his Northern Campaigns.

Trajan. A bust at Ostia, which invites comparison with Canova's Napoleon.

Plotina, wife of Trajan, a bust in the Vatican Museum.

Moesia, he had met an astrologer who had said the very same thing. Hadrian was now, at the age of twenty-one, a figure of national importance, as his brother officers were not slow to recognise. The ward of the heir to the throne could clearly be of great influence in helping or hindering their careers. They therefore sent him off to carry their congratulations to his cousin; and Hadrian found himself transferred, or seconded, to the XXIInd, the Original Loyals, who were then stationed in Upper Germany. Nerva, meanwhile, had sent Trajan a letter in his own hand and embellished with a quotation from Homer, saying that he had had him appointed *caesar* by the senate. This name had originally belonged to the great Julius. Augustus adopted it (he was Julius' great-nephew and heir), and so it became one of the "royal titles". When Vespasian became emperor he conferred it upon both his sons, Titus and Domitian, as a mark that they were his heirs *to the principate*. Thenceforth, until the time of Antoninus, the titles *augustus* and *imperator* were reserved for the emperor, that of *caesar* being conferred also on his heir or heirs—a convenient distinction.

Within three months, on 25th January, A.D. 98, Nerva died and Trajan was emperor. The whole thing had gone perfectly smoothly. Hadrian's hopes now beat higher than ever. Once again he hastened to congratulate his cousin, now sovereign of the Roman world. But once again he encountered the malignity of his brother-in-law, Servianus, who had succeeded Trajan as governor of Upper Germany. Trajan was at Cologne, in the neighbouring province. Servianus first of all tried to detain Hadrian on some pretext, and then when the lad insisted on going on, he arranged that his travelling-carriage should break down. Nothing daunted, Hadrian went on on foot. Trajan was pleased that his young cousin should have been so persevering, and was fonder of him than ever; but Hadrian never forgave Servianus. After all, had his mischief-making succeeded, Hadrian would never have been emperor. Even now he was not absolutely sure how he stood with Trajan. He therefore did what any intelligent Roman of the time would have done, he consulted the Virgilian oracle, already an established practice in his day and one which was to last until that of Charles the Martyr-King of England. In each case the poet was a true prophet, in Charles' case of doom, in Hadrian's of felicity. He lighted on the passage in the Sixth Aeneid, referring to Numa, the Roman king, as the man who is to be advanced to great authority, *"missus in imperium magnum."* That could mean only one thing, the greatest of all. An oracle in Asia supported the omen. Finally, through the good offices of a member of Trajan's staff, he was unequivocally established as Trajan's favourite. For the young man from Italica, the sun now shone from an unclouded sky.

Chapter IV

THE HEIR PRESUMPTIVE

BEFORE leaving Cologne the new emperor wrote a letter to the senate, in his own hand, in which he assured the conscript fathers that he would not execute, nor disfranchise, any honest citizen. There were to be no more heads of freeborn men exposed in the Forum, after secret killing without trial. From the first, Trajan made it clear that he would rule with justice and moderation. He did, nevertheless, put to death the officer and men of the praetorian guard who had mutinied against Nerva. Nerva was his "father", whom he was bound to avenge, even though the insurrection had failed, and had, in fact, been the direct cause of Trajan's being proclaimed heir. The praetorian guard was the emperor's own guard: it must be made plain at the very outset that the emperor commanded them, not they the emperor. The new Augustus then visited the Danube, to assure himself that all was secure on that frontier, and only in the summer of the year 99 did he move south to Rome. He took Hadrian with him.

Hadrian was now twenty-four, and it was high time he was married. It was Trajan's wife who arranged it, for in those days as in these match-making was a favourite feminine pastime. Plotina had taken a fancy to Hadrian. She had no children of her own, and Hadrian "filled the room up of her absent child", though one chronicler suggests that her affection for him was more like that of Phaedra for Hippolytus. The wife Plotina chose was a great-niece of the emperor, that is a young girl called Sabina, the daughter of L. Vibius and Matidia, herself the daughter of Trajan's sister Marciana (see Table II). Hadrian had little inclination for the match, but he knew how imprudent it would be to oppose Plotina. And so the wedding took place. It ensured two things: first, that for many years to come the empress, in the person of Plotina, would be Hadrian's ardent patroness, secondly, that he would be tied to a woman whom he did not love and who in turn came to hate him. Fortunately, as her portraits shew, Sabina was a listless, feckless woman (Plate 5): that tight little mouth displays a weak velleity that would never shew itself in open opposition. She indulged in *outré* fashions, specially in coiffure

—one of the foibles of the well-born Roman matron—but she stuck to Hadrian, and he tolerated her.

The new reign was inaugurated with the happiest auspices. Trajan was unceremonious and affable. He was attentive to business, and rewarded citizens according to their merits. To the senate he was correct and dignified, to foreign ambassadors he shewed every courtesy, treating them as though they, too, were Roman senators. When he was off duty he liked to drop in on his friends, or if he met them when he was out driving he would stop the carriage and ask them to join him. In Italy he encouraged municipal infant welfare centres. In Pliny's words, he restored to Rome not only the security of life but the dignity of life as well. Plotina well knew how to second him in this policy. She too, played the citizen. When she was entering the palace for the first time, she turned round at the top of the stairs, and, addressing the populace, said: "I am going in here just the same woman as I hope I shall be when I leave." Throughout Trajan's reign, which she survived by five years, she never lost the favour of the people. They must have made a very charming royal couple, the best that Rome ever had.

The seventeen years which followed were to be those of Rome's greatest military glory. Wider still and wider were her bounds to be set, by a series of victories which for brilliance and scope were not to be equalled until the days of Belisarius. Today, when the Roman Empire has long since gone the way of all empires, the great column which Trajan erected in the new forum which he built in the capital still unfolds to us the tale of that glory. It was during these seventeen years that Hadrian grew to maturity, from a youth of twenty-five to a man of forty-two. He was to share in these great achievements, but only as a junior; they were not his. He knew that only to Trajan could the renown of conquest ever belong. That knowledge sharpened his resolve to excel in the arts of peace. But meanwhile he must pursue his official profession. Almost at once, he had a lesson in the envy of mankind. Hadrian was a provincial. As a boy he had seen Rome at its worst, and he was not likely to be seduced into overmuch conformity with its fashions. He shewed this, as some men have done since in similar circumstances: he wore a beard. In ancient times men had worn beards. But in Rome beards had gone out in the later days of the republic. In particular, no emperor had ever worn a beard. For Hadrian, therefore, to sport one, was to flout convention. The reason given later was that that he wanted to look like a "philosopher", but, says the *Life*, he really did it to hide a natural scar on his face. Now it is true that on some of Hadrian's busts, though not on all of them, a scar is clearly traceable, running from the left-hand corner of his mouth diagonally towards his chin: the beard did *not* hide the scar. Besides it was a light beard, not a long philosopher's beard. The real reason for it must have been that Hadrian saw no point in carrying on a custom which he thought to be ridiculous. For in those days, as we know well from the pages of Hadrian's fellow Spaniard Martial, shaving was a prolonged torture. With no soap, and no steel, it was as clumsy as it was painful, even amid the comforts of the capital. How could a man be expected to shave when in the country, and, if he wore a beard in the country, why not in the town? So Hadrian reintroduced the beard. But the innovation, as it was accounted, can hardly have pleased the "older set". They decided to shew Hadrian what they thought of him. In the year 101 he had been appointed quaestor, that is an officer of the emperor's secretariat. One of his duties was to convey the ruler's messages to the senate, and to read them for him. Trajan found this convenient, because, although he held learning in the highest regard, he himself was a man of little formal education. One day, as Hadrian read, the senators started to titter —they were laughing at his provincial accent. Hadrian took the lesson in good part, and set himself, as Demosthenes had once done, to polish his accent and his style until they were fluent and easy.

Almost at once, Trajan undertook the first of the great campaigns which were to occupy him intermittently until his death sixteen years later. In all of them Hadrian took part.

The wars fall into two clearly defined spheres and epochs, as follows:

The wars in Dacia (Romania):	First 101-2.
	Second 105-6.
The wars in the Levant:	Annexation of Arabia (i.e., Trans-Jordan) 106. The war against Parthia (Iraq and Persia) 113-15. Jewish revolt in Cyrene 115. Further revolt in the Levant, including the Jews, 116.

Our information about all these campaigns, despite their magnitude and their importance for the history of the empire, is lamentably scrappy (see Sources and Acknowledgements). In any case, they are so remote both in time and space that it is difficult to understand them. For the purposes of this study, it will be enough to indicate their main incidents and consequences. To take the Dacian wars first.

What had happened is this. When Trajan visited the Danube frontier immediately after his accession (see page 35) he found the frontier quiet, but the general situation far from satisfactory. Domitian had to deal three times with turbulence and disorder on this frontier, and three times he visited it in person. He finally made a settlement with a Dacian king called Decebalus, by which, in return for a subsidy (or bribe), Decebalus undertook to keep the peace. As invariably happens when a man accepts a bribe as a regular source of income, in return for services to be rendered regularly, he very soon regards himself as an injured man, as being required to do too much for too little. So it was with Decebalus. Trajan at once saw that Decebalus was longing to start fighting again, and that the money was being wasted. A new road was constructed on the westerly approach to Dacia, along which, in the year 101, the Roman forces moved. Decebalus, who realised that Trajan was a very different man from Domitian, retreated. He joined battle near what is now the Iron Gate pass, and, although the Romans claimed a victory, the issue was indecisive, and Trajan had to be content with maintaining the Banat during the ensuing winter, when the Romans did not usually campaign. They had, however, to repel a raid which the hardy tribesmen made by swimming the Danube. The Romans, too, therefore learned to swim the Danube, even in winter, and among them the athletic Hadrian. Decebalus despatched two embassies to sue for peace. The first was sent back, the second found the terms too stiff. The war went on. Trajan was determined to take the Muhlbach fortresses, and after some hard fighting he succeeded. When the last stronghold, the Muncel Cteate above the Varosviz river, had fallen Decebalus capitulated: the scene is represented on the great column in Rome.

Trajan's terms were lenient. Decebalus was to demilitarise his country, to accept a Roman garrison, to return all Roman deserters and not to enlist any more. He was to remain king.

38

Decebalus had no intention of keeping these mild conditions. One by one he disregarded them. Finally, he encroached upon the territory of one of Rome's protectorates, the Iazyges, whereupon war was once again declared. This time there were to be no half measures. Trajan's chief engineer and architect Apollodorus, a Greek from Damascus, built a great bridge across the Danube at what is now Turnu Severin. It was a remarkable work—twenty stone piers, a hundred and fifty feet high from the base, the spans being a hundred and seventy feet, and the width of the roadway sixteen. Decebalus' allies, who had never seen anything like it before, melted away. By a pincer movement, Trajan converged on Decebalus, and in the summer of 106 again entered his capital. Decebalus committed suicide. The war was over. Dacia had ceased to exist as such. Many of the inhabitants had been killed, fifty thousand were led south in chains to meet a gladiator's death in the Roman circus. The goldmines were exploited for the benefit of the Roman treasury. Orientals moved in, and the gods of the Levant with them.

Hadrian had seen with his own eyes how a Roman army was organised, how it fought, how its commander conducted himself, compassionate to his own troops—Trajan had torn up his own clothes to supply dressings for the wounded when the supply of bandages ran out—ruthless to the enemy. He had seen, too, how a new province was organised, how it could be exploited for Rome. Hadrian had been on Trajan's staff and had lived on terms of intimacy with him. In after years he used to say the reason he got on so well with Trajan was that he was able to drink glass for glass with him: he knew how to humour him, in fact, as any sensible subaltern would. Between the two wars Hadrian served as clerk of the senate, and then in 105 he was nominated tribune of the people. It was the recognised step between quaestor and praetor. Originally it had been a plebeian office, whose holder could veto legislation which seemed oppressive. He was the people's guardian, and in the later republic the tribunes had been the labour leaders of the day. Under the empire, the appointment had no actual authority, but its emotional prestige was still strong. Even emperors, ever since Augustus, had held "tribunician power" and dated the years of their reigns by it. Only patricians were exempt from what was in origin a plebeian office, and that exemption Hadrian could not claim. When the second Dacian war broke out, Trajan appointed his ward to be commanding officer of the 1st, Minerva's Own, and took him with him to the war. Hadrian greatly distinguished himself. He now received from Trajan a very significant present. The emperor gave him a diamond ring which he had himself been given by Nerva. The gift recalled the precedent set by Augustus himself. When, in 23 B.C., he lay desperately ill and was not expected to recover, he sent for Agrippa, his most trusted minister and son-in-law, and formally handed him his signet-ring, the ring with his emblem of the sphinx on it, as an indication to everyone that Agrippa was to succeed him. For Hadrian now to become the possessor of a ring which had belonged to two emperors in succession could mean only one thing. In the following year he became praetor, whereupon Trajan found the sum of two million sesterces, about twenty thousand pounds, to enable Hadrian to provide "games" for the public. The following year he was appointed governor of Lower Pannonia, or Eastern Hungary. In this capacity he found, as many a governor has found since, that he was called upon not only to restrain marauders from beyond his borders, in this case the Sarmatians, but also to curb the pretensions of the army and the rapacity of the treasury officials. Hadrian was confronted with this triple problem, and we are told that he grappled with it so successfully that he was promoted to the highest office of all. He became consul. He was only thirty-three. It was while he was consul, says his biographer, that Licinius Sura, a fellow-Spaniard and one of Trajan's most trusted generals, told him that he was to be adopted. *Was* to be; but why was he not adopted? There he stood, the ward, the favourite, the nephew by marriage of the emperor, who had given him the symbolic ring—it was perfectly obvious that he was to be the successor. And yet he was not nominated as such. Why? Nobody knows the answer. Trajan may well have shrunk from a step which he knew would antagonize still further certain officers, and those near to him, and on whom he depended, who could not stand the sight of Hadrian. Secondly, people in the prime of life (as they think) are often reluctant to make any sort of will or testament, and a formal adoption was just that. Even old Nerva had required a mutiny to force his hand. Thirdly, Sura, who would probably have arranged the matter, died within two years.

But Trajan was fonder than ever of Hadrian. He was his

private secretary now, and wrote all his speeches for him. And in the year 112 came a by-no-means empty compliment from overseas. The people of Athens elected Hadrian their *archon*, or ruler, for they were technically a "free" city. They had never elected a foreign commoner before (and only once had they elected an emperor, Domitian, in 85), and would certainly not do so merely out of liking for Hadrian. That they now elected him is clear proof that they knew which way the wind was blowing. The Greeks usually do, and set their sails accordingly. They knew that their prescience would be rewarded, and so it was to be, richly. This election is the clearest indication that we have that by this time Hadrian was generally, and not only in the imperial circle, regarded as the heir.

As is usual, men worshipped the rising star rather than the setting sun. Hadrian was now clearly lord of the ascendant, and the best and wisest in Rome made sure that he would count them as his friends. Plotina saw that this association of her protégé with a particular set, however brilliant, would do him no good when he became emperor. Trajan, despite his sixty years, was about to set out on yet another campaign, this time in the east. It would be well if he took Hadrian with him, and appointed him governor of the key province of Syria. And so it was done.

Two questions must now be answered. First, why did Trajan attack Parthia? Secondly, what was the outcome of his campaign? To the first question the answer is twofold. The Euphrates is one of the few natural frontiers of the inhabited world. To the west of that river, although the customs of the orient may prevail, the policies, creeds and conventions of the West find acceptance. Beyond it, they do not. To cross the Euphrates is to pass the boundary between a world in which Greece and Rome have for centuries been paramount into one in which they never were. This great division was as real in Trajan's day as it is in our own. Old as were the glories of Greece, the grandeurs of Rome, in the land of the Two Rivers and beyond there had long flourished still older cities and men. Herodotus had written about them, and of their threat to the Mediterranean. Was not that true also of Egypt? It was, in a way. Egypt was ancient, and opulent. But even at the epoch during which Herodotus had visited Egypt, it was the Persians who ruled her. On the other hand, Egypt had never ruled the Persians, and had for centuries been an appanage first of the Greek Ptolemies and now for more than a hundred years of Rome itself. Persia, in the form of Parthia, was still very much alive, still an active menace. Never could a Roman forget the awful day in 53 B.C., when those same Parthians had utterly overthrown a Roman army. Parthia was a hereditary enemy. That was the first fact.

The second was that Trajan had every reason to suspect that Parthia had been in league with Dacia, that they had signed some sort of mutual assistance pact. That was why in 111 he had taken the government of Bithynia under his own administration, and had sent there as his legate his trusted friend Pliny the Younger. The letters exchanged between them have been preserved, and are one of our most precious sources of information about Roman provincial government. The Dacian wars had shewn Trajan the dangers of compromise, or half measures. He was determined to finish the Parthian question once and for all.

The course of the Parthian war belongs to the history of Trajan, not of Hadrian. As a prelude to it, Armenia was occupied. The main objective now lay open. The Parthian capital was at Ctesiphon, a few miles south of modern Baghdad. Its capture by Trajan was greeted with rapture by the senate, and Trajan eagerly pushed on down the Tigris to what is now Basra. There, gazing to the south over the waters of the Persian Gulf (for the coastline was much farther north than it now is), Trajan exclaimed: "If only I were as young as Alexander, I would go to India and beyond!" But already he had overshot himself. The northern parts of the newly conquered territories were already in revolt:

"He was unable [says the chronicler] to keep what he had conquered. For his victories he was loaded with honours, and allowed to celebrate as many triumphs as he liked; but he kept on writing to the Romans about so many peoples he had conquered, that they were not able to take them in, or even get their names right. They were getting ready a triumphal arch for him, in his own Forum, and preparing other tributes, and had decided to go out to meet him further than usual, when he came marching home. But he was never to see Rome again, never again to come up to his previous achievements, to lose indeed what he had won. While he was sailing down the river to the Gulf and coming back, all the conquered districts were thrown into confusion and revolted, their Roman garrisons being either killed or expelled. It was at Babylon that Trajan heard of this. He had gone there because it was so famous, though he saw nothing there except mounds, storied friezes and ruins, and because of Alexander, to whose spirit he offered sacrifice in the room where he had died."

The scene might have come from a Greek play. Amid the ruins of Babylon, already a by-word for beauty made desolate, the Roman conqueror confronts failure where his Greek model had encountered death.

Trajan saved what he could. Leaving a makeshift client-kingdom in the south of Mesopotamia, he was able to hold Armenia (now eastern Turkey) and northern Iraq. He turned aside to besiege Hatra, that strange sculptured stronghold in the desert west of Mosul. He failed to take it, as Septimius Severus was to fail. The sun, the flies, added to the general discomfort. Trajan, already an ailing man, turned "his majestic grey head" to the west. He returned to face disaster domestic and foreign: Antioch, his headquarters, had been destroyed by an earthquake the year before, but he must perforce spend the winter of 116 in the ruined capital. Then came the news that the Jews of Cyrene, Egypt and Cyprus, even those of Mesopotamia itself, had revolted, massacring thousands of their gentile fellow-citizens. Further afield, the Moors, the Britons and the Sarmatians were all shewing signs of restiveness.

Such was the outcome of the great Parthian campaign.

Trajan realised that he must go back to Rome, and for Rome he set out, leaving the army of the east in command of Hadrian, who was still governor of Syria. The Parthian campaign had wrecked Trajan's health. He was suffering from dropsy, then he had a stroke which left him paralysed. He got as far as Selinous, now Selente, on the coast of Turkey opposite Cyprus, and there collapsed. On his deathbed he at last formally adopted Hadrian. As he could not write, the documents were signed by Plotina. Hadrian heard of his adoption, at Antioch, two hundred and fifty miles away, on 9th August, 117. Two days later he learned that Trajan had died on the 8th. Hadrian was emperor. He was forty-two.

Chapter V

HADRIAN'S ACCESSION

HOW wise Plotina had been, how far-sighted! If Hadrian had been anywhere other than at Antioch, had he held any other post than governor of Syria, at the time of Trajan's death, it is more than probable that he would never have succeeded his uncle as emperor. Being where he was, he was nearer to the dying Trajan than any possible rival and, equally important, he had under his command the army of the east, that is to say five complete legions, out of a total of thirty, together with detachments from at least four more. The rest of the army was distributed about the frontiers of the empire, chiefly in the north. Hadrian therefore commanded the largest army in existence to be found at any one station within the empire. He needed this support, for two reasons. First, there was the widespread revolt to be put down. Secondly, there were his personal enemies to be overcome.

Of the revolt in the east, particularly as it affected the Jews, it will be necessary to go into some detail in a later chapter (XVIII). It is enough to record at this stage that Hadrian's general, Turbo, was able to restore order in the whole of the Levant, and that in a few months. As always in that region, the absence of an army, and the news, no doubt with the usual exaggerations, of its reverses and retreat, had stimulated the more ardent antinomians, who beat an automatic retreat when the army reappeared, intact and unbeaten. But in committing the task to Turbo, Hadrian had overlooked another general, Lusius Quietus. Quietus was a Moor, a sinister but competent man, who, after crushing the Jewish revolt in Mesopotamia, had been governor of Judaea. Hadrian now disregarded him and even took away some of his troops for service with Turbo. Quietus passed over to the ranks of Hadrian's enemies.

These were already many and powerful.

At once they began to make trouble. Their first line of attack was that Hadrian was not really emperor at all. Trajan, they said, had intended to nominate an elderly lawyer called Neratius

44

Priscus. Priscus was a member of the privy council, and a friend of Pliny; but at seventy he could hardly be expected to cope with the cares of empire. Trajan may very well have said to him, as was now recalled, "If anything happens to me, look after the provinces"; but to interpret such a general remark as an intention of adoption was nonsense. Others claimed that Plotina had simply forged the letter—overlooking the fact that Trajan being paralysed could not write—and said that Trajan had meant to send a message to the senate suggesting a few possible names, or even that, like Alexander, whom he had invoked on his Parthian campaign, he had intended to leave no heir at all, or even that Hadrian had only been adopted posthumously, by a trick of Plotina's, who smuggled someone into the death-chamber to impersonate the emperor, speaking in a feeble voice. This sort of rubbish was bandied about, in the usual manner of bazaar rumours, and was even current two generations later. Unfortunately, the only independent witness who could have settled the matter once and for all, Trajan's personal valet, who was only twenty-eight, died four days after Trajan, whether from natural causes or not has never been determined.

Conjecture weighed as nothing against the whole tenor of Trajan's conduct towards his ward for years past. It is only significant as shewing how willing Hadrian's enemies were to prove, if they could, that besides being an outsider he was also an usurper. Technically, it is true, Hadrian should have waited for confirmation by the senate. But that would have taken more than a month, and what was to happen to the authority of Rome in the meantime? Hadrian took the only possible course. He wrote a modest letter to the senate, explaining the circumstances, asking for their approval, and assuring them that he would do nothing contrary to the public interest, and would not put any senator to death. He asked for divine honours for Trajan. He also cleverly declined in advance any honours the senate might wish to vote for him such as "father of his country", on the ground that Augustus had not won the title until a quarter of a century after he had been proclaimed Augustus. He also refused the triumph which the senate offered him, saying very fittingly that it should be Trajan's; and so it was the dead emperor's effigy that graced the triumphal chariot, and also the commemorative coins. This self-effacement looked like policy—to hamstring the malignants who might have

45

tried to withhold the usual honours. But in fact it was genuine; throughout his career, Hadrian always preferred, as we shall see, to give honour to others rather than to assume it himself.

Having despatched the letter to the senate, and arranged for the chastisement of the rebels, Hadrian set out from Antioch to pay his last respects to Trajan. The corpse had been burned and the ashes placed in an urn of gold. Hadrian now held a memorial service, and sent the urn off to Rome, in charge of Plotina, his mother-in-law Matidia, and Attianus his guardian. On arrival in the capital the ashes were placed in the pedestal of the column which still dominates the Forum of Trajan.

Hadrian returned to Antioch, where he handed over the government of Syria to Catilius Severus, a man of like tastes with himself, a bit of a philosopher, and a close friend of Pliny the Younger. He himself was to be consul twice and prefect of the city, his great-grandson the future emperor and philosopher Marcus Aurelius. Hadrian had chosen his successor in the key position with care and wisdom. He wanted his reign to shew from the outset what sort of man he was and what sort of men he trusted. To win the people, he ordered the distribution of a largesse of three golden guineas a head even before his arrival, just as to the army he had given a double donative. He went further. It had become the custom in the last days of the republic to contribute money for the purchase of gold wreaths (in imitation of laurel) to be worn by successful generals at their triumphs. At first voluntary, these contributions soon became compulsory. Since, under the empire, only emperors might celebrate triumphs, these "benevolences" came to be levied at the beginning of the reign, and were known as "coronation money". Augustus had remitted the levy, but his immediate successors do not seem to have followed his example. Hadrian now remitted the contribution due from Italy, and reduced the sum due from the provinces, at the same time making it clear that he was not recouping himself from the treasury, which had been almost drained by Trajan's wars. Unfortunately, his guardian, Attianus, did not possess Hadrian's tact. The zealous old watchdog wrote to his ward and said that he strongly recommended the immediate execution of three men. The first was actually prefect of the city, the second one of Trajan's generals and a close friend of his who had twice been consul, but later, having intrigued against his benefactor,

46

had been banished to an island. The third was a prominent aristocrat of an ancient family, who was known to have plotted against both Nerva and Trajan. Nerva had banished him and his wife to Tarentum, Trajan to the greater security of an island. They were a dangerous trio, no doubt; but Hadrian refused to allow their execution. One of them, Crassus, was, it is true, killed "while trying to escape", but the others lived on. Attianus thought that Hadrian was weak. The next plot would have to be dealt with differently! Encouraged by the new emperor's leniency, it was not long in coming.

Hadrian was still on his way to Rome, but he had already made it clear that he favoured a policy of "peace, retrenchment and reform". At the time of Trajan's death there had been plans for the reconquest of the whole of Mesopotamia. Hadrian would have none of it. He abandoned all Trajan's conquests east of the Euphrates. He allowed the Parthians to reassert their authority, under their own king; and he compensated the makeshift monarch whom Trajan had installed (see page 43) by giving him a principality in Kurdistan. Armenia, too, was allowed to have its own king once more. The reason for this withdrawal was primarily strategic: the Syrian desert interposed far too real a barrier, logistics became too impossibly overstrained for Mesopotamia to be controlled from Syria, a geographical postulate which is still valid today. But there was another consideration as well. As has already been noted (see page 41) the Euphrates is one of the world's natural cultural frontiers. Judaism had already discovered that: it had returned from the exile "beyond the river" very different from what it had been when it first went east. Seven hundred years later, Islam was to do exactly the same: Shi'a belief and practice are as different from that of the western Sunnis as the architecture of Persian Islam is from that of the western branch. Hadrian, with his quick, sensitive mind, had realised this fundamental divergence, and the innate cultural strength of Persia. Ever since he was a boy at Italica, where the Phoenician and African influence was so strong, he had mistrusted all that was un-Roman and un-Greek. Here in the Levant, he had already seen and heard enough of the east, even in this "Greek" metropolis, to make him dislike the city and its people. He had no intention of exposing the empire to a still stronger infection of the foreign. He saw, with prophetic far-sightedness, that if Rome tried to absorb Asia, Asia would end by absorbing Rome.

In the north, the case was different. Hadrian may have wanted to abandon Dacia, he may even, as we are told, have given orders to dismantle Apollodorus' famous Danube bridge; but the process of colonisation and exploitation had already been carried so far that to abandon Dacia would have meant abandoning a number of Roman settlers. This dilemma has confronted later imperialists more than once; but in Dacia, at least, there was no clash of cultures, and so the province was retained. Besides, it was rich in natural resources and produced gold. Hadrian would appeal to secret instructions which he said he had received from Trajan, just as Augustus used to say he was only carrying out the wishes of the great Julius. In neither case could anyone contradict, even though in both they doubted. Still, to make sure that Dacia was administered just as he wanted it to be, Hadrian appointed his trusted Turbo to an extraordinary command, equivalent to that of the prefect of Egypt, that is to say outside the administrative machine, and dependent on him personally. It included the whole of the Danube provinces, Dacia and Pannonia. Dacia was later divided into two provinces, of which the lower one was committed to a procurator, or civilian governor of the second class, with no legionary command. This shews how prosperous and peaceful the territory had become. Meanwhile, the Roxolani, the tribe who lived at the mouth of the Danube, were shewing signs of rebellion. Their king complained that his "subsidy" had been reduced—the standard complaint of "protected" chiefs—and that he was "oppressed". Hadrian at once went to see him, pacified him, and then at last pressed on to Rome. Before he could reach it, two new plots had been uncovered.

The first was the work of Cornelius Palma and Publilius Celsus, men who had held important offices under Trajan, and in whose honour statues had been erected. They had always hated Hadrian, and had even tried to jockey him out of the succession. They now proposed to get rid of him during one of his hunting expeditions, when an accident could easily be arranged. The second plot was the work of Avidius Nigrinus, a man of consular rank who had been a provincial governor in the days of Domitian, and was now, we are told, destined by Hadrian to succeed him. He allowed his impatience to get the better of him.

Sabina, wife of Hadrian, a bust in the Vatican Museum.

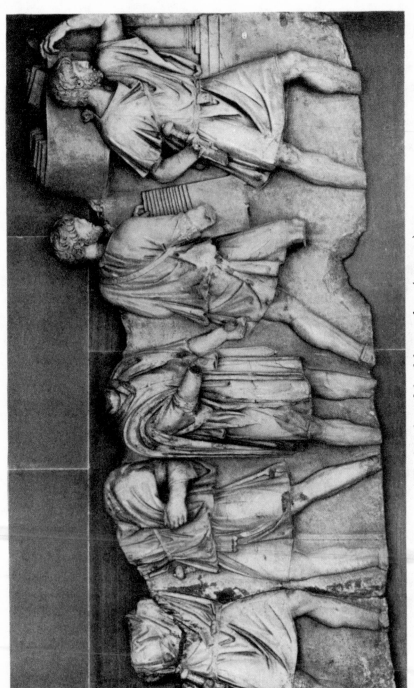

The burning of the debt-vouchers (page 49).

In the disgruntled Lusius Quietus he found a ready accomplice, and it appears that others joined in the conspiracy. Hadrian was to be assassinated as he was sacrificing, just as Galba had been on the way to the same ceremony, fifty years before. Attianus got wind of both these plots. The conspirators were warned, and at once dispersed. But they did not escape. The senate was dragooned into passing sentence of death. Palma was caught at Tarracina, on the coast south of Rome, Celsus at Baiae, Nigrinus at Faenza, and Lusius "on the journey homeward". All were killed.

When Hadrian heard the news, he was, as he recorded in his lost autobiography, appalled. Such summary measures ran clean counter to his policy of moderation. At the same time he was shrewd enough to see that the existence of such plots was proof of his unpopularity and that the execution of the plotters would only increase it. Leaving the trusty Turbo as his lieutenant in the north, Hadrian made all haste to Rome. He reached it on 9th July, 118, eleven months after his elevation. He was coldly received. It was thought, naturally enough, that it was by his own orders that these four eminent men, all of consular rank, had been put to death. Hadrian went down to the senate and assured them of his ignorance and innocence of what, after all, they themselves had authorised. He swore never to punish a senator except in pursuance of the verdict of a senatorial court. Hadrian was determined that bygones should be bygones, and did all he could to let his former enemies know it. Meeting one of them soon after his return to Rome as emperor, he greeted him with a smile. "You have escaped," he said. He personally directed the distribution of a second largesse to the populace. He went farther. He decided to cancel all the debts owed to the imperial treasury. He wrote off the equivalent of almost a million sterling, and had the vouchers publicly burnt in the forum of Trajan (see Plate 6). He also ruled that a similar relief was to be offered every fifteen years. He renounced his claim to the estates of executed persons, making it over to the state, a step as clever as it was generous, since it meant that he could never again be accused of having any financial interest in the death of a citizen. On his birthday, in the year 119, he provided a magnificent spectacle in the circus, in which two hundred lions and lionesses were killed. For the future, he said, he would allow the senate to vote games in his honour at the public expense only once a year, on his birthday. Even then, he would contribute a thousand wild beasts. On other occasions he gave gladiatorial combats for six days in sucession.

He extended Trajan's infant welfare centres. He provided regularly-paid maintenance grants for poor but deserving men, and women, too. Those senators who had become poor through no fault of their own he assisted with grants-in-aid, in the form of family allowances, so that they could sustain the dignity of their rank. The requisite capital qualification for a senator was not high, only ten thousand pounds. A champion jockey was worth more.

Hadrian did all he could to conciliate the senate. He always attended their regular meetings if he was in Rome or in the neighbourhood. He took his consulship seriously, and often administered justice during the four months for which he held the office in 118 and 119. His table and his carriage were alike open to his friends, be they senators, knights or even freedmen. He liked to visit them in their own homes, and when they were ill he would call to enquire, and to cheer them up, as many as three times in a day. He treated his brother-in-law Servianus with correct deference, always going forward to greet him; but he would not serve as consul with him, because Servianus would be the senior of the two, and that was more than Hadrian could stomach. Attianus, the emperor realised, must go: to keep on as prefect of the guard the very man who had procured the death of the four senators would look like condoning their execution despite all his protestations. The slanderers said that Hadrian would have liked to kill Attianus. He wished nothing of the sort; but since he could not dismiss a prefect of the guard—there were two of them—the office being of no stated term, and often held for life, he induced his old guardian to resign, and then gave him senatorial rank, the highest decoration, he tactfully remarked, it was in his power to bestow. Since Nero's day this had been the recognised reward for retired prefects. It did not entitle them to sit in the senate, but they had official precedence with senators of consular rank, and wore the toga with the broad purple stripe that was their insignia.

The other prefect was an attractive character called Similis. He had worked his way up from the ranks in Trajan's army, and always kept the popular touch, even though his statue proclaimed his merits to the whole town. He had never wanted to be prefect, and now saw an opportunity to retire. Hadrian begged him to stay on, but the old man had his way. He retired to the country, and there spent the remaining seven years of his life. He had the following inscription placed on his tomb: "Here lies Similis, who existed so-and-so many years, and lived seven."

In replacing these two officers, who held posts so vital to the emperor's own safety, Hadrian shewed how sure, and also how misleading, his instincts could be. Turbo naturally was the first choice. As we know from an inscription discovered in Syria in 1952, Turbo had had a varied and distinguished career. He had been an officer in the city guard and in two regiments. He had been in charge of the posts and he had been admiral at Misenum. In this last capacity, he would have come into personal contact with Trajan during his eastern campaigns, and so with Hadrian, too. They were old friends. He had fulfilled his task on the frontier, which had been a temporary appointment, and it was natural that he should now return to the capital. He was a most zealous and loyal officer. He gave himself no airs, he was always on the job. He spent the whole day at or near the palace, and would go his rounds even at midnight. He was never seen at home during the day, even when he was ill. Once when Hadrian begged him to take a little rest, he replied with the old soldier's quip that Vespasian had used: "A prefect ought to die on his feet." For Turbo's confrère, Hadrian chose one of his literary friends: it would be nice, he thought, to have an artist on the domestic staff. So Septicius Clarus was appointed. He was a well-known littérateur, and it was due to him that the Younger Pliny, as he himself says, was induced to publish his letters, for which we must always be grateful to Clarus. He was also the friend of Suetonius, the famous author of the racy *Lives of the Twelve Caesars*, who now held a court office as imperial secretary. Unfortunately, their good fortune went to the heads of the two literary men. They grew familiar, and treated the empress with less respect than court etiquette demanded, and both were dismissed.

Hadrian's attitude to women was equivocal. He was suspected of seducing the wives of his brother officers, and of carnal association with males. He made no pretence of any love for Sabina, and was known to say that had he not been emperor, and therefore required to set an example, he would have sent away his wife, whose ill-temper and tantrums were unbearable. But as empress he demanded that she be respected. When his mother-in-law died, in 119, he honoured her memory with gladiatorial games (an odd form of commemoration, even for a mother-in-law), by the distribution of spices and the issue of special coins, in which the "deified mother-in-law Matidia" is seated in a temple between statues of victory. So far as the general public was concerned, he decreed two other measures to conciliate the matrons of Rome. The first concerned the circus. Nero had introduced, as an attraction and diversion, the practice of throwing free lottery tickets among the spectators. They were little wooden balls, and were thrown at random into the crowd. Each one was inscribed with the gift to which it entitled the holder, anything from a slave or a horse to a piece of plate, or even a good joint of meat. Titus had continued the practice. The pushing and shoving which such a distribution caused in the packed theatre may be imagined. Hadrian now ordained that the coupons for the men and the women were to be distributed separately.

His second enactment in favour of women was that the public baths should be reserved for their exclusive use during the mornings. Hitherto, women had been constrained either to bathe in promiscuity with the men, or to stay away. The new régime ensured that during the mornings the men would be encouraged to work, and the women left free to gossip and bathe unmolested by man. How they must have blessed their new emperor.

Chapter VI

THE IMPERIAL PLAN

HADRIAN was now not only emperor, but safely emperor. The frontiers were calm: in the north, the Dacian bastion protected the eastern end of the boundary, a pacified Britain and a quiet Germany the west. In the Levant, revolt had been suppressed, Trajan's embarrassing oriental adventure liquidated, and the *limes* firmly established on the desert fringe of the new Arabian province. In Rome, too, the new emperor had promoted tranquillity. His justice and generosity had won over the army, his affability and munificence the people. With the senate he could not pretend to be popular, nor with the clique of Trajan's marshals. But both they and he knew that with the praetorian guard in the hands of Hadrian's tried nominees, it would be folly to attempt to unseat him.

Hadrian was thus free to develop his imperial plan. Of what did this consist? It is at this point in the story of Hadrian that we come up against the enigma of his character, because at this vital juncture our written sources, thin as they are and compiled so much later, become almost silent, so that we must proceed by inference from coins, monuments and documents which have an indirect bearing on Hadrian. Nevertheless, it is possible to make a fair general assessment of what Hadrian set out to do. In the first place, as an indication of what he was *likely* to feel, we must put his own heredity. He was a Roman, but he was not born in Rome. He had no sympathy for the remnants of the old patrician society of the capital, not that it was very old or patrician now. Many of the more effete families had died out (for, despite all that Augustus had tried to do to counter childlessness, it had become not only common but even fashionable), and most of the more vigorous had fallen as victims of the jealousy of a Caligula, a Nero or a Domitian. Hadrian knew from his experience that the provincials were a far lustier stock, and that both in literature and in administration they had already proved it. What better Roman had there ever been than his own uncle Trajan?

53

Secondly, Hadrian had seen more of the Roman dominion than any former emperor had done at the time of his accession. He knew not only Spain, but France and Germany, the Danube lands, Asia Minor, the Levant and Mesopotamia, and thus had a personal acquaintance with the imperial patrimony that no one else in Rome could rival. He realised that these provinces were capable of development, as we should say nowadays, but also that they still lived a life of their own, which they had a right to enjoy. Hadrian's aim was to make this possible. He therefore regarded the empire not as a collection of chattel-provinces, but as a family of sister nations. It would be going too far—very much too far—to think of Hadrian as a "Commonwealth man", because our conception of representative government was unknown in antiquity; but Hadrian did believe that, while Rome should always be chief, and the provinces subordinate, all those provinces, including Italy itself, should regard each other as equal, and all be bound to the emperor not as to a master by fear, but as to a father by love.

Such was the Hadrianic idea. It was not wholly new: few political theories are wholly new. The title *pater patriae*, "father of the fatherland", was old in Roman usage. It had been honourably bestowed and borne in the days of the republic. Cicero had gloried in it, when in 63 B.C., after defeating the Catiline conspiracy, he was so hailed. Augustus had accepted the title in 2 B.C. to mark the twenty-fifth year of his principate. Tiberius never held the title officially, though flattering inscriptions accorded it to him. Other Julio-Claudian emperors allowed about a year to elapse after their elevation before they adopted the style. It had become almost a formality for the senate to bestow it on the emperor. But Hadrian took this notion of the emperor's fatherhood seriously: he saw himself as father of the equal *patria* of the whole empire. He therefore refused the title when it was offered to him on his accession, and again later. It was only in A.D. 128, when he had been emperor for ten years and felt that he had earned the designation, that he accepted it.

By a strange historical chance, we have the means of checking, or "controlling" to use a modern term, this development of the idea of the emperor's fatherhood. In the year 100 Pliny the Younger was elected consul, and in September of that year he delivered in the senate a speech of thanks for his election. He took the opportunity to deliver a "panegyric" on his friend, the then reigning emperor Trajan, who had himself recently undertaken a consulship. The speech is devoted largely to contrasting Trajan's virtues with Domitian's vices, in a strain of emetic flattery: nevertheless, there are, amid the servile verbiage, some grains of fact. (Once, when Pliny spoke for five hours on end, the emperor, with tactful self-consideration, several times begged the orator not to overstrain his voice, but Pliny went bravely and relentlessly on.) Pliny is able to quote actual examples—such as Trajan's relief measures for Egypt when the Nile's inundation failed—to shew that he is a kindly prince, not a grasping tyrant, a father not a master. The following passage from the peroration is worth quoting, both because it shews this aspect of Pliny's meaning, and also because it furnishes clear proof (sometimes overlooked) that in Rome, on the very morrow of Hadrian's marriage to Trajan's great-niece, it was expected and even hoped that he would succeed his great-uncle as emperor:

Pliny is invoking the great god Jupiter Capitolinus, and says:

"It is thou, who speaking by the mouth of the emperor hast declared thy judgment, and hast vouchsafed to him [i.e. Nerva] a son, to us a father, to thyself a supreme priest. Now therefore unto thee do I with full trust and confidence make the same prayers and supplications which our sovereign lord [princeps] bids us make on his behalf: first I beseech thee that, if he govern the republic well, and for the common good, thou mayest be pleased to preserve him unto our nephews and great-nephews; and that finally thou wilt grant unto him a successor born of his seed, formed by him and made like unto his adopted son, or, if this be forbidden by fate, that thou mayest direct his choice, and mayest shew unto him one worthy to be adopted in the Capitol."

In such a speech, in such a peroration, the proviso about the good government of the *respublica*, for the common good, is all the more telling: only on such terms was the divine blessing to be accorded to the emperor.

Corroboration of this conception of the father-ruler comes from another orator, a Greek this time, who also addressed orations to Trajan. His name is Dion Chrysostom, of Prusa in Bithynia. He was an orator and sophist who had been banished by Domitian and restored by Trajan, whose close friend he became. In the first of his *Sermons on Sovereignty*, which seems to have been addressed to Trajan about the same time as Pliny's panegyric, Dion gives a picture of the good king. "Not only has he the right to be called Father, as a word merely, of his citizens and subjects, but to make the title good by his deeds. *Master* he cannot bear to be called not only by free men, but even by slaves; because he regards himself as ruling not for his own selfish ends, but on behalf of mankind in general." And there is much more in the sermon in the same strain. Again, in the third sermon, Trajan is, very significantly, contrasted with the Persian king, much to the advantage of the Roman, who rules in equity, not by caprice.

For the reign of Hadrian, we have unfortunately no comparable literary evidence. But for the age of Titus Antoninus, his successor, we have. A famous Greek orator, Aelius Aristides, visited Rome about five years after Hadrian's death, and delivered an oration in praise of the city. It is addressed to Rome, not to the emperor, though there is, as courtesy demanded, a polite reference to him in the peroration. To the Greek, brought up on the idea of the city state, the city is a more abiding concept of perfection than its ruler-for-the-time-being. Yet Aristides, like Pliny and Dion, expresses the same views about the *objects* of empire; only, these views are all the more striking because they now describe not an ideal but an existing state of affairs. Rome rules the world. It is the centre of every activity. "Egypt, Sicily and the civilised part of Africa are your farms." "What the Atlantic means to you, the Mediterranean meant to the Persian king." And what was sovereignty in the days of the Persians? "It was a contest to slaughter as many people, to expel as many families and villages, and to break as many oaths as possible." How different is Rome: better even than the Greek republics of old, "for the Athenians and the rest of the Greeks were good at resisting aggression, and defeating the Persians and spending their revenue for the public good and putting up with hardship, but they had no training in government, in which they proved failures". In this enormous empire—so much larger than any earlier one—which stretches from Ethiopia to the Black Sea, and from the Euphrates to Britain, "Neither seas nor the lands between are bars to citizenship, and Asia is treated exactly the same as Europe. In your empire, every avenue of advancement is open to everyone. No one who deserves office or responsibility remains an alien. A civil world-community has been set up as a free republic, under a single ruler, the best ruler and teacher of order. Everybody comes together, as into a common forum, so that each man shall receive his due." For Rome, the centre of the world, diffuses security throughout it, an unobtrusive power "compared with which the walls of Babylon were mere child's play and women's work". It is the legions, loyal and disciplined, that assure this, because "Mars has never been slighted by you: he dances his ceaseless dance along the banks of the outer rivers, and so saves bloodshed". In fine, "to praise the empire properly would need the whole life of the empire, and that is eternity".

It is a wonderful picture, which even at this distance of time excites a glow of admiration, a nostalgic wish that our own epoch, too, might witness such felicity, such brotherhood, that men might travel, safe and unmolested by thieves or frontiers, from Newcastle to Baghdad, and from Khartoum to Odessa. But then, behind the pleasant vision comes always the haunting question, "Was it worth it?" Was it really possible to surrender independence, "freedom", in order to share such bliss? This question has troubled mankind since man emerged as a political animal. For Englishmen, and those who throughout the world have imitated the polity of England, it was regarded as an axiom, for the two centuries and a half which followed the Glorious Revolution of 1688, that the answer must always be no. It was (as usual) Edmund Burke who put the case most clearly, when speaking of the American colonists:

"As we must give away some natural liberty, to enjoy civil advantages; so we must sacrifice some civil liberties, for the advantages to be derived from the communion and fellowship of a great empire. But, in all fair dealings, the thing bought must bear some proportion to the purchase paid. None will barter away the immediate jewel of his soul. Though a great house is apt to make slaves haughty, yet it is purchasing a part of the artificial importance of a great empire too dear, to pay for it all essential rights, and all the intrinsic dignity of human nature. None of us would not risk his life rather than fall under a government purely arbitrary."

Thus Burke states the English position. But it has not been adopted at all times and in all places. There have been subjects of empires, of the Ottoman, of the Austrian, of the British, even of the French or Russian, who were happier, sometimes, though by no means always, than they have since become under "free" national governments. Islam, which commands the allegiance of millions, has always inculcated submission: the very word means *surrender*, that is to God. The great organisation which is in so many ways the successor of the Caesars, the Roman Catholic Church, insists that complete obedience is the natural condition of the Christian soul, and in this view of human destiny millions throughout the world ardently concur. They submit to a pontiff as sovereign, and they, like their secular predecessors, address that sovereign as father, he them as his children. That Hadrian should have attempted to establish an empire based on equality in submission, and governed for the general good by a father-sovereign, is by no means so vain an end as it has often been regarded among uncatholic nationalists.

There was, moreover, another influence which worked upon the minds of men in favour of monarchy, originally and most powerfully in the eastern provinces, but now increasingly in the west as well: the memory of Alexander the Great. From the time of his death, in the year 323 B.C., Alexander had become a hero of legend. His achievements, his meteoric rise and eclipse, above all his fraternal internationalism, had implanted in the hearts of mankind the image of a godlike innovator. Alexander had believed in equality; he really had tried to found a bi-racial empire. He himself had married a Persian, and at his urging ten thousand of his officers and men had done the same. Alexander had died at the age of thirty-two, and his empire had been broken up into fragments; but the kingdoms which his marshals consolidated from parts of his conquests endured, that founded by Seleucus in Syria for more than two hundred and fifty years, that by Ptolemy in Egypt for three centuries, until the days of Augustus himself. The capitals of these kingdoms, Antioch and Alexandria, were the second and third cities of the empire. Alexander had thus bequeathed a legacy of which the lustre still awed and attracted the Romans. The farther the old republic receded and the closer became the bonds which attached Rome to the east, the brighter shone the lode-star of Alexander and his conception of kingship as the head of an ideal and equitable society. Hadrian, the Greek enthusiast, well understood this: he would emulate Augustus, but he would profit by the Alexander myth as well. He still called the Roman state a republic, when in fact it had become a monarchy: the English still call their state a monarchy, whereas it has for some time and for all practical purposes been a republic. In each case it is the sovereign head that engages the hopes and the affections of the subject.

Chapter VII

THE BOND OF EMPIRE

THE sting of Aristides' tribute to Rome lies in its tail, in the assertion of the eternity of Rome. *Aeternitas Populi Romani*, "The Eternity of the Roman People"—Vespasian had put the slogan on his coins, and what emperors put on their coins was of the first importance.

It must be remembered that in antiquity there were no newspapers, no photographs, none of our own vaunted and insidious methods of influencing public thought. The only means, therefore, of saying anything more than once, quickly, and to a large number of people, was the coin.

It has been aptly compared, in that respect, to the modern stamp, which like the Roman coin, can carry a slogan, or make known a policy, or commemorate a *fait accompli* with the maximum speed and effect. The Roman emperors used their coins for just this purpose. Fortunately for us, many of them have survived, so that they have become one of our most precious sources of historical information. We know many things from coins of which we should otherwise be ignorant. The imperial coins also give us the most accurate representations we have of the features of Roman rulers. Roman portrait sculpture of the first two centuries was, it is true, exceptionally fine. In the opinion of a great art historian, Bernard Berenson (who died recently), it is not until the Renaissance that comparable representative work is to be found; but the official bust was in those days as in these not seldom a slight improvement on nature, whereas the coin, which was to be widely circulated, tended to be more accurate, if only because in the capital it could be compared by so many with the original.

The coin, therefore, had a vital political part to play. Hadrian, following precedent, advertised his policy and acts through his coinage. One of his very first issues bore the word Adoption, and shewed Trajan and him clasping hands. Then there was one which proclaimed The Liberality of Augustus, with a scene of him distributing largesse. Another commemorates his Remission of Nine Hundred Million Sesterces of Debt, and so on. The idea of the durability of Rome naturally comes in for illustration. He hit on the telling idea, which had occurred to none of his predecessors, of putting the actual date on a coin in terms of years since the city's foundation. If a city had existed for eight hundred and seventy-four years, surely it had a good chance of continuing? It was clever psychology. It seemed indeed to be The Golden Age which another issue announced.

But Hadrian knew quite well that something other than propaganda was needed to bind his empire together, something more even than gratitude for money, bread and circuses. He saw that the bond must be spiritual. Here, he was faced by a profound problem. What were men to believe, to fear and to love? All men, not only Romans, but Greeks and Syrians as well? Hadrian, we are told, had a great respect for the gods of Rome, and hated those of despised foreign cults. He always himself performed the duties of *pontifex maximus*, or high priest of the national gods. Thus in religion Hadrian appeared to be a conservative, just as he did in his literary tastes. He used to say that he preferred Cato to Cicero, for instance, and Ennius to Virgil, which was like saying that Langland is a better poet than Milton. It was the same with historians: he preferred the old to the modern. On the other hand he used to say that Homer was not so good as a much later and almost unreadable epic poet called Antimachus. Which leads us to the conclusion that Hadrian, when discussing authors, sometimes expressed provocative views just to see what would happen. That he really did appreciate Virgil will be seen from a touching incident of his last days. But when it came to religion, he certainly would not trifle: too much was at stake. Nevertheless, it is baffling that Hadrian should have taken up the position he did, and for the following reason. The religion of Rome had long ceased to satisfy the best minds in Rome. It is extremely hard for a modern, with so many centuries of monotheism behind him, to grasp the ethos of an age when monotheism in its Jewish and Christian expressions was the guide of minorities only. To reconstruct the feelings and aspirations of those minorities, even though we are their heirs and are the possessors of the scriptures which are, as it were, our title-deeds, even that is hard enough. But to comprehend what were the religious emotions or experiences of the majority is almost impossible. What was their conception of godhead, of the divine, for instance? What were the right relations between man and divinity?

Gibbon, in an oft-quoted passage, dismisses Roman religion with characteristic flippancy: "The various modes of worship which prevailed in the Roman world were all considered by the people as equally true; by the philosopher as equally false; and by the magistrate as equally useful." The passage is worth recalling in order to shew how completely an eighteenth-century "rationalist" could misunderstand ancient belief: each one of his three statements is the reverse of the truth.

There were still, in the second century, simple folk who worshipped the antique deities of Etruria or Latium, who still sought the protection of Priapus for their flocks and gardens, the succour of Lucina in childbed, the bounty of Vertumnus for their harvests; just as today their descendants solicit the benevolence of the saints who have succeeded to their shrines. Some, too, both in town and country, may still, from force of habit, have experienced a sense of reality in venerating Jupiter, Mars and Venus. But such souls were in a minority.

It is a commonplace to say that "traditional religion had lost its hold on the educated Roman of the second century", but before we can judge what this meant, it is necessary to know just what that hold had been. How did the average Roman, as opposed to the simple peasant, or indeed the ancients in general, conceive of his deities? It is perplexing, for instance, to read that the emperors, or still more an Antinoüs, were *deified*, that ordinary men were to be regarded as gods, and that they were then to be qualified by the same adjective, *divus*, as in Renaissance Latin was applied by the Catholic Church to *saints*. To attribute to the Roman emperors the same status as that of the Christian saints, as something far less than the Persons of the Trinity—even that is to rate them too high. The best definition of the relationship between the pagan gods and their human servants is probably that given to his friends by the late Professor Dawkins, frivolous though it may at first sound. He used to say that the gods were "Upstairs", human beings "Us below stairs". The difference between the two was one of class, not kind. Those below served those above, for certain wages. Apart from general protection, they did not expect much from them otherwise. The servants might criticise the masters as much as they liked, and they were not really surprised at their little lapses, even if they involved an occasional seduction of a maid or a footman from below.

To abandon such an earthy relationship was not to abandon very much; and it is not to be wondered at that many Romans did so, and yet kept up the old forms. It was not, as it might at first seem, hypocrisy or cynicism. It was simply that there was really so very little to give up, spiritually speaking, and the old forms were not much more than what we should now call folklore, or traditional ceremonies, such as survive, because they are loved, harmless and picturesque, in many parts of Europe and the British Isles.

This was the attitude of the majority of decent Romans; but for a growing number of sensitive men and women this negative attitude was not enough. Something else, something more vital, was necessary. Some sought to find it in philosophy. Polite Rome had long been familiar with the Greek schools, with the doctrines of Pythagoras and Heraclitus, of the Stoics and the Epicureans, of Plato and Aristotle. A few rare spirits, such as Marcus Aurelius, did find in philosophy a guide to right living, bleak though it might be. But in general Greek philosophy made no deep appeal to the Roman mind. For one thing, it was too subtle: the Roman was a practical man. For another thing, the Latin language—as the Christian fathers and doctors were in their turn to find out— is not capable of expressing nuances of philosophical ratiocination. Cicero's so-called "philosophical" works we may read for their style, but hardly for their contents. It is the same with Lucretius, the great materialist philosopher-poet of the republic, of whom the late Monsignor Knox said that he had "a genius for irreligion". His poetry has moved and inspired generation after generation of other poets and ordinary men and women: his philosophy provokes nothing but a good-natured smile.

Philosophy, therefore, except for a very small number of men, who must be able to acquire it through Greek, and to whom the Greek idea of being was superior to the Roman, was no answer to the enquiry. Philosophy compared to religion is like a battery compared to a dynamo: it can give only what it has received, it is not a prime mover. In the second century, mankind increasingly craved a *personal* guide, a *personal* hope, in one word, they sought *salus*, a word which originally meant simply *health*, in the bodily sense, but which, in the period of which we are treating, came increasingly to mean the health of the soul, that is, *salvation*.

Where was salvation to be found? It was to be found not in the West at all, but in the East. In the words of Carcopino:

"One great spiritual fact dominates the history of the empire: the advent of personal religion which followed on the conquest of Rome by the mysticism of the East. The Roman pantheon still persisted, apparently immutable; and the ceremonies which had for centuries been performed on the dates prescribed by the pontiffs from their sacred calendars continued to be carried out in accordance with ancestral custom. But the spirits of men had fled from the old religion; it still commanded their service but no longer their hearts or their belief. With its indeterminate gods and colourless myths, mere fables concocted from details suggested by Latin topography or pale reflections of the adventures which had overtaken the Olympians of Greek epic; with its prayers formulated in the style of legal contracts and as dry as the procedure of a lawsuit; with its lack of metaphysical curiosity and indifference to moral values; with the narrow-minded banality of its field of action, limited to the interests of the city and the development of practical politics—Roman religion froze the impulses of faith by its coldness and its prosaic utilitarianism. It sufficed at most to reassure a soldier against the risks of war or a peasant against the rigours of unseasonable weather, but in the motley Rome of the second century it had wholly lost its power over the hearts of men."

It was oriental mysticism that won them. The new religions came from the Levant, from Asia, above all from Egypt. There were dozens of them. None of them made exclusive claims—it was simply a matter of choice. Some were more popular than others. Attis from Phrygia, Cybele from Asia, Mithras from Persia, were among the smartest; but it was the Egyptian deities which made the deepest appeal. They were so very ancient, the land they inhabited was so august, so fertile, so mysterious that they seemed to be more truly and essentially gods than any of their rivals. Serapis, Osiris, Isis, all these deities were acclimatised in Rome and in her empire. So powerful was Isis that for many generations Christians and Jews would bear the name Isidore, or gift of Isis, as easily as Theodore, gift of God. All these cult stimulated religious emotion, and bestowed a sense of personality, of a stake in a future existence, on their adherents. Unfortunately, besides spiritual assurance, they also encouraged carnal excesses. There were recurring scandals in Rome occasioned by the hierophants of these alien cults, and from time to time one or other of the strange gods was "banished", but they generally contrived to get back, such was their hold on the Roman mind, Their attraction is summed up by Cumont as follows:

"The oriental religions by appealing at one and the same time to the senses, the reason and the conscience, gripped the entire personality. They seemed to offer, by comparison with those of the past, more beauty in their ceremonies, more truth in their teaching, a higher standard in their moral outlook. The splendid rites of their festivals, their devotions, now grand, now moving, sad or triumphant, captivated the mass of the simple and lowly. The progressive revelation of an antique wisdom, inherited from the old and distant orient, won the minds of the educated. The emotions which these religions stimulated, the consolations which they offered, chiefly attracted women: it was in them that the priests of Isis and Cybele found their most ardent and most generous adherents, their most enthusiastic propagandists. Mithras, on the other hand, gathered round him only men, on whom he imposed a rough sort of moral discipline. Every soul, in short, was vanquished by the promise of spiritual purification, and the infinite vista of eternal bliss."

Among these oriental cults there were two which require special notice, because they were to prove by far the most potent and enduring, and one of them was wholly to change the basis of the Roman polity. They are the only two of all those religions that flourished then which still flourish today, the two monotheistic cults, Judaism and Christianity. Of these two religions much more will have to be said at a later stage. Here it is only necessary to record that they had already found a home in the capital, where in the eyes of the Romans they were two among many others. It was the startling discovery that these two religions were wholly different from all others that caused such consternation: in the easy-going eclecticism of Roman religion, it was the exclusiveness of Judaism and Christianity which shocked, not their doctrine.

What was Hadrian's attitude to religion? What cult would he choose to be his bond of empire? He was said, as has been noted before, to be a scrupulous observer of the old Roman rites, and a contemner of all alien beliefs. The second half of this statement is not wholly true. In fact, it was in Hellenism, in a romantic antiquarianism, that Hadrian imagined that he had found his spiritual mansion. But, at least after his visit to Egypt, he was also attracted by the Egyptian religions. Hadrian was clever enough to realise that the old Italian pieties would not move the peoples of the north or the west or the south. Clearly, the only cult that could unite the whole empire was that of Rome itself. That must everywhere be encouraged. If, in the east, the emperor, as the embodiment of Rome, were also treated as a god, and called a god, no harm would be done.

To the monotheists this attitude was blasphemy, and in this fact lie the seeds of Hadrian's struggle with the Jews. The Christians he never really understood: he was not interested in them.

Hadrian's spiritual imperception was to prove his tragedy. He was to accomplish so much, for so many. But in the end he was to be frustrated and to fail. Despite all his efforts, it was not to be the faith of Hadrian that would perpetuate Rome as the Eternal City.

Chapter VIII

THE NEW MODEL

THE last two chapters have shewn, it is hoped, that Hadrian was an innovator, that he had conceived a new form of polity, namely the empire as a family of provinces, the happy and prosperous children of the Mother City, and that he intended that the veneration of that city, and of himself as its lord, should be the spiritual bond of empire. But Hadrian, the artist, the dreamer, was also a hard practical administrator: he knew well that if his idea of empire was to prevail, it must be demonstrated to the inhabitants of the empire on the spot, and that the demonstrator must be himself. Secondly, he knew perfectly well that he must tour the provinces, not as an artist, but as a man of affairs. He had always before him the dreadful example of another emperor who had tried to shine as an artist on tour, Nero. It would never do to alienate his already suspicious subjects by seeming to be "superior", to know more than they did: he had no wish to share Nero's fate, nor to see his whole plan founder through mishandling. In this mixture of the artistic temperament and a gift for practical affairs, Hadrian resembles another brilliant prince who was regarded as an alien innovator, and disliked accordingly, namely Prince Albert, the consort of Queen Victoria; but, unlike the Prince Consort, Hadrian was solely responsible for the fate both of himself and his policy.

There would be exceptions to the general rôle in which he had cast himself, exceptions for exceptional places, namely Athens and Egypt. But, for the rest, it was to be Hadrian as *augustus* and *imperator*, not Hadrian "the versatile dilettante" (as his biographer calls him) that the provinces would see. *Augustus* was a title that Hadrian particularly loved. It linked him with *the* Augustus, the great founder of the empire. He had now been dead long enough to have become a legendary hero, a sort of King Arthur figure, and to aspire to imitate him was the most laudable manner in which an emperor could hope to win his subjects. That Hadrian succeeded in doing so, and that his success seems to have surprised his people, is the inference to be drawn from a series of *Remarks*, thirteen in number, which have come down to us. They are little tags, little administrative decisions, none in itself important, but all tending to shew that Hadrian was, when conducting business, not only the trained, that is to say cautious, civil servant, but also the humane father of his people. The first tells of a young man who came to the emperor and said he wanted to enlist in the Guards, "How tall are you?" asked Hadrian. "Five foot six, Sir," answered the lad. "Serve two terms in the City Foot, and then for your third [when the boy would be, if not six foot, at least somewhere near it] you can transfer to the Guards." Another petitioner approached the emperor with the request that his father should be recalled from exile. This was a serious matter: Hadrian hated harsh measures, and the man might have been a victim of Domitian. At the same time he might not: he might be a genuine malignant. "Who exiled him?" he asked the man. "The prefect, Sir," he answered, meaning the prefect of the city, one of Hadrian's most trusted officers. "Let me see the file," he replied, then added: "But mind you come and see me again." In yet another case a man claimed that his father had been wrongly fined, and deprived of a large portion of his property. He told the sad tale at some length. "When did all this happen?" asked Hadrian. "Ten years ago, Sir," said the man. "Well, why didn't you go and see the prefect and put your case to him before? It's all your own fault. If we are going to dig up and re-try old decisions, be they right or wrong, we shall never get to the end of it."

Two more examples will be enough. One day a man came to Hadrian and said, "My lord, my sons have been called up." "Good," replied the emperor, "that's fine." "But they're only ignorant boys, and I'm afraid they'll do something out of line [*extra ordinem*], and then where shall I be?" "Don't you worry, said Hadrian, "they're only going to do peacetime service." "Oh please, lord emperor, send me instead, or let me go as their servant, so that I can look after them." "God forbid," said Hadrian, "that I should send you to wait on your children. You be a centurion, and then you can be their N.C.O." Finally, once when Hadrian was distributing largesse to some soldiers, a poor woman cried out, "Lord emperor! Please tell them to give me an allotment from my son's share! He neglects me, he does!" At which the son exclaimed, "I don't recognise this woman as my mother." "In that case," said the emperor, "I don't recognise you as a Roman citizen."

These little encounters, so vivid, so trivial and human—they must have touched the people who first heard them, as being the sort of thing they did not expect to hear from Caesar, but how glad they were that they did, that he really was the wise, gentle man they had hardly dared to hope he might be. Each of the scenes might, word for word, have taken place in the office of the best type of British colonial District Commissioner, whose highest praise and guerdon it is not to receive decorations from above, but to be hailed as father from below.

Such was the ruler who, in the year 121, set out on the first of the empire tours which were to make him famous, and to scatter over the empire benefits and buildings of which the relics still, after eighteen centuries, adorn the world in which he moved.

Before Hadrian could leave Rome—and only he knew for what an extended period he intended to be absent from it—he decided to overhaul the administration and to reform the army, for these were the twin instruments whereby his new imperial plan was to be made real.

As his pattern he adopted Augustus, and more and more he seemed to grow into the part. Moderation—that was to be his watchword. As Weber points out (*Cambridge Ancient History*, Volume XI, page 306), Hadrian's coinage is a significant illustration of this aim. In official inscriptions and dedications, Hadrian is given his full list of titles, right down to the end of his reign, and the cities of the east often added flattering additions or variants. But on the emperor's own coins the full official titulature occurs only in the first year. After that, first *imperator* is dropped, then even *caesar*. Up to the year 123, he is *pontifex maximus* (the one title that the Popes have inherited from the Caesars), holder of the tribunician power, and "thrice consul", having held that office again in 119. For the next five years the coins proclaim him simply as *Hadrianus Augustus*. After that, he added *pater patriae*, father of his country, the title which he, like Augustus before him, had declined until late in his reign, and again mentions the third consulate.

Like Augustus, Hadrian now set out to refashion the machinery of the state, while leaving the façade untouched. He left the senate alone. The senate was still a very important body. During the nineteenth century it was fashionable to decry the senate of imperial days, to scout it as an assembly of frightened sycophants, cowering before the imperial despot, because during that century it was the republic and not the empire that was lauded and held up for imitation. But the senate still continued to be a repository of administration and legal power right through the whole life of Rome, to such an extent that when in the fourth century Constantine founded his New Rome in Constantinople, he was bound to create a new senate there as well. To this day, the College of Cardinals is officially styled, in canon law, the senate of the Roman pontiff. Hadrian shewed all respect to the senate. He made friends of its most prominent members, and liked to be seen in their company. He was scrupulous in maintaining their dignity, He always stood to receive a senator. Once, when two senators were leaving his house, a slave (no doubt one of "Caesar's household", the civil service,) slipped in between them and started to walk off with them. Hadrian at once sent a messenger to give the slave a clip on the ear and to tell him not to presume to walk with men whose property he might one day be. He often attended meetings of the senate and liked to assure the assembled fathers that he would so govern that they should know that the state belonged to the people, not to him. He chose the senators with great care. If they were poor, through no fault of their own, he paid them family allowances. He always sought the senate's approval for important appointments, even to his own council.

The senate was no longer exclusively Roman. Indeed, it was predominantly provincial. "Hardly three of the old Roman families were still to the fore," says Weber. Men from Gaul, from Asia, or, like Hadrian, from Spain, men who represented the new cosmopolitan commonwealth, these now made up the senate. They were given plenty of work to do, and they were respected by their emperor; but it is significant that only to two of them did Hadrian entrust a third consulship, to match his own, and they were his nearest relatives, his brother-in-law, and Annius Verus, an old Spanish friend, and grandfather of the boy he adored and hoped to have as his successor.

The second order in Roman society was that of the *equites* or knights, men of sound standing, financially and professionally, the upper middle class of Rome. Of this order, too, Hadrian set out to enhance the responsibilities, and to define the status. To start with, it must be clear that they were inferior to the senate, and must not encroach on the prerogatives or prestige of senators. Senators were to be called *"clarissimus"*, "excellency", as we might say; knights *"eminentissimus"*, "right honourable". Nor might any knight ever sit in judgment on a senator, even as a member of the privy council, which contained both senators and knights. But within the bounds of their own order, the duties and influence of the knights were greatly increased. The civil service was to be their domain. Formerly, state business had been transacted through a secretariat of freedmen. This system had led to every sort of abuse. The freedmen of Claudius and of Nero became bywords for corruption, peculation and intrigue, designed to advance the interest of themselves or their creatures. Hadrian decided to put an end to the whole system: if he was to be absent from the capital, it was vital to leave the administration in clean and faithful hands. Besides, to enhance the status of the knights was one more step towards his provincial partnership policy. Many provincials nowadays became knights, and the sons of those knights might become senators. So this broad-based secretariat, this civil service open to talent, came into being. There were several chief secretaries, and each had his own department, correspondence, finance, supply, wards in chancery, death duties, treasury counsel, crown lands. Another key post which was now in the hands of a knight was that of city prefect. When the emperor was absent from Rome, this officer practically replaced him so far as the capital went. The public postal service was also reformed. This was not a postal service as we understand the term, but a service of vehicles, drawn by relays of horses, which carried official despatches, and officers of state, or privileged guests, over the famous Roman roads. Originally the expense of this service had fallen on the municipalities through which the roads passed. Nerva remitted it for Italy. Hadrian now placed the system under the control of a special prefect, a knight like the rest, and made its upkeep a charge on the treasury.

In these reforms Hadrian shewed great sagacity. The creation of a civil service which offered an honourable and well-paid career to a man of talent, from whatever province of the empire he might hail, must certainly have helped to weld the imperial fabric yet more surely into one. At the same time, the fact that the bureaucracy was appointed by and bound to the emperor alone, enhanced his power and authority. He had taken nothing from the senate; but he had given himself a good deal more.

Hadrian viewed his military commitments wholly in terms of the frontier. No longer, as in his uncle's glorious days, were the legions to go forth conquering and to conquer, they were simply to guard Rome's boundaries, and to ensure that Rome continued to hold what Rome had held. Hadrian had started his career as a soldier; he knew the frontier, and he knew how hard it is to maintain the discipline and morale of an army at peace, as he intended that his should always be. There was no doubt that discipline had grown slack, and that loyalty, as the more recent history of his country had shewn, had become dangerously volatile—it might be given not to Rome, but to whatever general seemed most likely to reward it. This had to be remedied. Once again, Augustus was invoked: the legions must be led back to his spirit. The "Discipline of Augustus", that was the slogan with which the coins proclaimed the reforms. The soldiers were well paid, Domitian having raised the rates by a third. Hadrian insisted that the pay must be earned. Officers were appointed and promoted for efficiency, not popularity. Leave was granted sparingly and in accordance with regulations only. The ordnance department was overhauled, obsolete equipment was got rid of, new and improved designs were introduced. No officer was allowed to accept a "present" from a soldier. The mere fact that this regulation was necessary shews how flabby discipline had become. Men were not to be enlisted below age, nor kept on the strength when they were too old for active service, both profitable methods of pocketing public funds. The camps, too, were reformed. The military stations inevitably attracted unofficial faubourgs, and in these the soldiers had constructed canteens and recreation-rooms, and had laid out fancy gardens, as soldiers always do. All these superfluities were proscribed by the new regulations, and the camps were restored to their purely military functions.

These rigorous measures met with no opposition. On the contrary, the army was confirmed in its loyalty to Hadrian. Wherever he might be, in no matter how remote a corner of his dominions, he never to the end of his days had to fear the slightest wavering of his troops' devotion. If Hadrian was a disciplinarian, he was a generous one, and he offset the severity of his régime with a judicious bestowal of bonuses and decorations. Above all, he knew his men personally, or at least as many of them as he could. When he was in camp, he shared the bacon and sour wine of the legionaries. He marched with them, twenty miles at a time in full armour. He wore ordinary active service kit. He refused to wear a sword belt with gold or jewels on it, and was reluctant even to have an ivory-handled sword. He would visit the soldiers in hospital, and made a point of getting their names right. He used to choose the camp sites himself, and personally selected candidates for promotion, even down to the rank of centurion; so surely did Hadrian base his reforms, that they were still in force a century and a half later.

There is another, more controversial, aspect of Hadrian's military policy of particular interest to the modern English reader, because a parallel situation has arisen in his own day. Hadrian felt that he must apply his theory of "partnership", of the equality of all the provinces, including Italy, to the army no less than to the administration. He therefore ordained, as a basic principle, that the army be recruited locally, that is to say from the sons of the provinces in which the various units were stationed —and Roman legions, unlike modern regiments, remained in the same region for years, more than a century on end sometimes. This meant, in effect, that there was no longer to be one *exercitus Romanus*, the Roman army, but a number of provincial armies, and by the end of the reign these armies were being addressed as such, "the army of Spain", "of Germany", and so on. The advantage of the system, apart from its consonance with Hadrian's theory of imperial partnership, was that it gave the inhabitants of a region a personal interest in the protection of their own frontiers. The danger of it was that regional loyalties might in time obliterate the bond of unity. Hadrian sought to lessen that risk by making the Guard the keystone of his military fabric. It was the *corps d'élite* of the army, a paragon of discipline and smartness. Its higher posts were reserved for Italians only, or men who were (like Hadrian) of Italic blood. Its officers were sent as instructors to the line regiments, who were constantly exhorted to model themselves on the traditions and standards of the Guard. The Romans, although the secondary grade of their social order were called *equites*, horsemen, or knights, never after 100 B.C. raised a military force of cavalry. This was always recruited from

Rome's "allies", whom Hadrian encouraged to maintain their individuality, granting them the privilege, for instance, of shouting their war-cries in their own vernaculars instead of Latin. Finally, just as in later empires, the frontier forces were recruited wholly from local populations, and remained an un-Roman militia.

Nevertheless, despite his reforms, there was one thing that Hadrian could not do, and that was to maintain the army at a strength adequate to the needs of empire. That was not Hadrian's fault. As will be seen, even in the days of Claudius there were not enough troops to go round: for the invasion of Britain, the Rhine-Danube frontier had to be dangerously thinned. Later on, the process was reversed, and part of Scotland had to be evacuated to provide troops for Dacia. To assemble an army for the Jewish war, units had to be drawn from all over the empire. There was no strategic reserve. This was partly from policy, lest its commander be tempted to make a bid for the purple, as had happened more than once before; but the chief reason was that the troops were simply not there. The *Pax Romana* had defeated its own ends when it came to the army. As Hadrian was to find out in his native province, men who had for so long known the blessings of peace had no intention of preparing for war—an attitude not unknown in later ages. Hadrian, far from being able to expand the army, found himself unable to maintain its existing strength. When he became emperor, there were thirty legions in the Roman army. During his reign, two were lost. They were never replaced.

Thus it came about that Hadrian had to depend more and more on two substitutes for the old army. The first was an increasing use of auxiliaries, local levies drawn from the tough populations of the frontier provinces; the second was the physical frontier, a material barrier, of which he was to construct several—the most famous of all being that in our own country.

Chapter IX

LAW REFORM

HADRIAN'S reforms of legal procedure and his codification of statute law were to constitute one of his most splendid and enduring memorials. In retrospect, scrutinised in the tranquil tomes of Justinian, Roman law appears as a serene, majestic unity. In its origins, on the contrary, it is fantastically complicated, far more so than the law of England, France, Switzerland or the United States of America. Three springs of legislation nourished the fountain of justice.

Originally, Roman law was statute law. That is the first spring. In the days of the republic it had been the Roman people, gathered in one of their various assemblies, which had enacted the laws. In imperial days two new sources were tapped: the senate, and the emperor.

The first attempt at codification was the *Twelve Tables*, in the middle of the fifth century B.C. Four centuries of law-making enriched and confused the original compilation. In English and American law, statutes are—in fact though not in theory—supplemented by judicial decisions, or case law. Precedents are created, and, as Disraeli put it, a precedent embalms a principle. The courts explain and transmit it. Roman law knew no such common-sense and convenient device. What happened was this: at the beginning of his year of office, the city praetor, the foreign praetor and the two aediles in Rome, and each governor of a province, issued a statement setting forth the principles on which he intended to administer the law during his term of office. This was called *edictum perpetuum*, perpetual edict, or *tralaticium*, because most of it was *carried over* from year to year. It was not, strictly speaking, perpetual, because although most of it was repeated every year, it was always open to a jurist of a different way of thinking from his predecessor to change details or to introduce refinements and new interpretations. The resulting uncertainty greatly benefited the lawyers, for even though in practice the city praetor's edict was accepted as the model, the ordinary citizen, specially in the provinces, which tended to look to the foreign praetor, could never be quite sure what the law really was. Over the years a huge new body of law came into being, generated almost haphazard by the praetorial and provincial edicts.

Under the empire, the old assemblies met no more except for purely nominal exercises, rather like an English cathedral chapter "electing" the Bishop who has been nominated to it by the Crown. It was the senate that had succeeded to them, and the decrees of the senate, the *senatus consulta*, which now had the force of statute law. These decrees were naturally previewed by the emperor; but the emperor himself was now the third source of law: he had only to issue a rule, or an opinion, or rescript to a question from a governor, and it was law.

The emperor issued his own mandates, the emperor controlled those of the senate: only one step was now necessary to make the emperor the sole fount and origin of Roman law—to regulate the praetorial edicts. Hadrian did this. As it happened, a plausible opportunity for so doing presented itself before he left on his first journey. As part of his plan for depriving Italy of her primacy, and reducing her to equality with the provinces, Hadrian appointed four circuit judges, one for each of the regions into which the peninsula was divided. If each of these four judges was to be allowed to introduce his own edict, in addition to those already current, chaos was bound to result. There was but one remedy: the perpetual edict, the fruit of all the perpetual edicts, must be codified. And so it was done. Among the members of Hadrian's privy council (whose duties, like those of our own, were predominantly legal) was a certain African jurist, from what is now Tunis, by name Salvius Julianus, generally known as Julian. He was a career civil servant, who in succeeding reigns held three provincial governorships and was twice consul. He was enormously industrious, and contrived to finish his codification in less than a decade. The senate ratified it, and the new code itself became part of statute law and endured until the days of Justinian. No other jurist ever had a more abiding influence on the shape and scope of Roman law.

Besides the three species of law already mentioned, now, by Hadrian's action, reduced for all practical purposes to one, namely himself, there was yet a fourth source of legal light—the jurisconsults. These were lawyers, selected for their learning and ability in exposition, whose official function it was to give opinions. If the panel gave a unanimous opinion, the judge was bound by it, but Hadrian ruled that where they differed the judge might make his own choice. This system has survived to this day: the muftis of Islam are the exact analogues of the Roman jurisconsults.

Hadrian's own legislation is of interest, for the light it throws on his character and methods. Sometimes he proposed measures to the senate, who accorded him the privilege of putting forward as many as he liked; but often he legislated by personal rescript.

His known enactments reflect that mixture of shrewdness and humanity which always seemed to be at odds within him, the shrewdness all too often degenerating into meanness, the humanity into sentimentality. Hadrian was a good financier. He always had all the heads and figures of the budget by heart, and he was the first to appoint a treasury counsel, to watch the interests of the privy purse. Yet his laws all seem to lean towards the citizen rather than the state. For instance, when men were banished, their whole estate had formerly been forfeit to the treasury. Hadrian allowed the children to retain one twelfth of it, or more if the family were large and indigent. He preferred, he said, to see the state increase in men than in money. He himself would accept no legacy from a stranger, nor even from a friend if the man had children of his own. Under his more rapacious predecessors, failure to leave at least something to Caesar had meant that Caesar took the lot. Hadrian had his own detectives, and very efficient they were; but he would have nothing to do with common informers. He simply would not hear any accusations of "treason", because he knew how the whole of Roman society had been curdled by the informers of earlier reigns. He took particular care of the young. He himself would select and appoint guardians for derelict orphans. He did much to lighten the lot of the slaves. The terrible labour-camps, to which both slave and free had formerly been sentenced, he abolished. No master was to kill his slaves: if a master had a grievance, the courts were there for its remedying. Formerly, if a master were killed by a slave, it was the horrible custom to kill all his slaves out of hand. Hadrian enacted that when such a crime was committed, only those slaves who were near enough to the scene to have been implicated were even to be arrested. He forbade the castration of slaves, and the selling of them, either male or female, to brothel-keepers, "except for some good cause". Nor might the boys be sold to be trained as gladiators. Torture of slaves was a recognized process of Roman as of Greek legal procedure. No slave's evidence was valid if obtained otherwise. Not even Hadrian could end this abomination. But he did his best to limit it, because he recognised that it was "untrustworthy and dangerous, and cheats the truth". Antiquity, as d'Orgeval points out, could at least, unlike our own age, boast that it was slaves only, and not free men, who were tortured to obtain evidence.

Municipal affairs were also a hobby of Hadrian's—naturally, since he wished to raise the status of city life throughout the empire. He accepted honorary office in more than one town, including, as we have seen, Athens (see page 41), and his own birthplace Italica. He paid Hadria, from which his ancestors had sprung, Naples, and other cities in Latium and Etruria a similar compliment. In Rome heavily laden wagons were refused entry into the city—a law whose revival many modern Romans must crave. It was illegal to ride a horse in a town. Senators and knights, whenever they appeared in public, must wear a toga, except when going home after dinner.

In so far as the army is concerned, his legislation was on the side of the soldier. The most important concession related to inheritance. At this period, soldiers on active service were still forbidden to marry. Logically, therefore, any children they begat had no existence in law. Hadrian realised that this was harsh and inhuman, and ordered that they were to be regarded as the heirs of their fathers.

The army, the law, the finances, the civil service—all had now been reformed and renewed. Competent and faithful officials were in charge of affairs. The capital was the seat of an efficient and stable government. Hadrian could now turn his attention to the provinces.

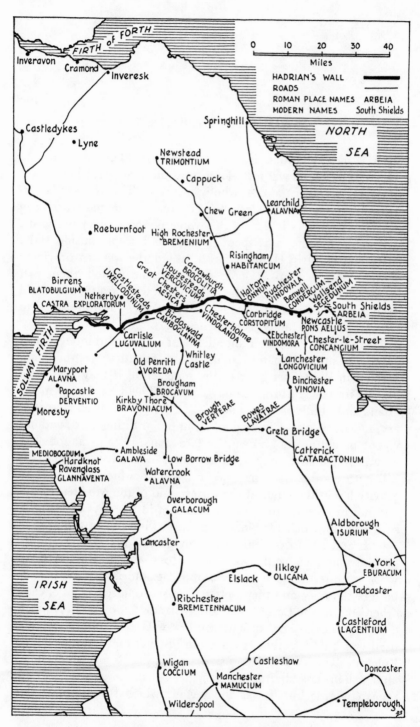

This map does not show all the Wall forts.

Chapter X

HADRIAN IN BRITAIN

THE most vigorous decade of Hadrian's life, from the year 120, when he was forty-four, until the year 131, when he was fifty-five, was spent almost wholly in travel. This in itself is surprising; but to the modern western reader the most arresting aspect of the tours is that of the whole period of over ten years, only one, the first, was spent in western Europe outside Italy. After that one trip Hadrian never visited the western provinces of his empire again. It looks as though he visited them first because he wanted to "get them out of the way", so that he could devote his time and energy to Asia and Africa, and above all to Greece. That, certainly, is what he did.

To a modern European this allotment of time and interest may appear disproportionate. To us of the twentieth century, still basking in the sunset glow of the nineteenth, it may well seem natural to regard Europe as having always held a primacy in the affairs and minds of men. The Levant, for us, has been a secondary, indeed second-rate, region, an imperial tilting-yard, without vigour or culture of its own. Of late years, oil and nationalism may have led us to pay more attention to the Levant; but it is still not easy for us to imagine an epoch in which the centre of gravity lay in the lands at the eastern end of the Mediterranean, and not in those at the western end. Yet in the days of Hadrian so it was, and had for long been. In civilisation, in the arts, in wealth and length of years, the provinces of the eastern empire far outshone those of the west. The second and third cities of the whole empire, Antioch in Syria and Alexandria in Egypt, were both of the east; and they were within six hundred miles of each other, so that the Levant was doubly irradiated by both. Antioch and Alexandria were ardent centres of Greek culture. Athens itself was linked to them by a chain of cities and islands such as Ephesus, Rhodes and Cyprus. True, it was Rome which now, after a long and destructive struggle, ruled the entire Mediterranean world; but it was the Levant which still supplied the

Hadrian's Wall, central section, looking west (page 87).

Britannia, with spear and shield, sitting on the Wall (?), in an attitude of defence—the forerunner of the figure on the reverse of the modern pennies and halfpennies. As Professor Grant has pointed out, this coin is unique among Hadrian's "provincial" series. Of these there are 30: 17 commemorate the "visit" of the emperor, and shew him clasping hands with a figure symbolising the province; 12 proclaim the "restoration" of a province, and depict a grateful figure kneeling before him. Only Britannia—the name is clearly legible beneath the figure—is represented alone and self-reliant, as she was so often in future to be.

creative ideas, the artists, the architects, and, above all, the religious faiths, by which men lived. Before Rome was, the Levant is. For Hadrian, the sensitive, enquiring artist, it was the east that held the lure; but for the soldier and emperor it was the west that held the more urgent duty, and that must first be done.

His first goal was the Rhine, the frontier he had known as a boy. Here the garrisons were inspected, and steps taken to ensure that the new regulations were enforced. Then, taking ship, Hadrian sailed down the river to the land of the Batavians, the ancestors of the modern Dutch, with whose cavalry Hadrian had swum the Danube as a subaltern. He admired them and decided to reward them. So to the south of what is now Leyden he founded a small settlement, and gave it his own name: *Forum Hadriani*, he called it, Hadrian's Market. The name, or half of it, survives today, in Voorburg. Thence he took ship to Britain.

Throughout the whole length and breadth of the empire, there was no nation which had given so much trouble as the Britons, except the Jews. These two peoples, so different in situation and outlook, never seemed able to see that submission was better than revolt, assimilation by Rome preferable to the stubborn maintenance of their own peculiar customs. Many a Roman must have wished that Rome had never had anything to do with either.

To the modern Englishman, Roman Britain has a strange and compelling appeal; it possesses the romance of the utterly remote. In Italy, France or Spain, even in parts of the Levant, Rome seems very near, and the daily life of today to be but a continuation of the Roman epoch. The language is predominantly Latin, the countryside is that which Roman poets have made familiar to us, and at almost every turn some vista, or some building, recalls an episode in Roman history or literature. Despite invasions, earthquakes and political changes innumerable, the land and the people are still Roman. To see the legend "S.P.Q.R.", *Senatus Populus Que Romanus*, the blazon of the republic's standards, on the side of a modern Roman tram, or even, in Palestrina, "S.P.Q.P." engraved over the tiny cemetery of what was once Praeneste, seems quite natural, the emblem of continuity. In Britain, this feeling is wholly missing, for two reasons. The first is that in Britain, Rome never really "caught on". No province of the empire except Dacia was wholly occupied for a shorter period

—only a little over three centuries—during which time Roman culture never struck deep roots, never spread evenly and deeply over the wild and pathless expanses of an inhospitable island. The second reason is that the cultural continuity of England has, since the departure of the Romans, been broken not once, but twice. First came the invaders from the east, the Angles, Saxons and Jutes. They brought with them their own culture. Not only did they evict the native inhabitants from their homes, hustling them off to cower in the west, in Wales and Cornwall, but they also obliterated their polity and culture. England became an Anglo-Saxon island. Then, in the eleventh century, came the Normans. The Norman conquest did not have the same radical effect upon the constituency of the population as the earlier invasions, but it did bestow on England a political and cultural complexion which has lasted to this day. Roman Britain, therefore, is the third layer from the top, insulated from us, and we from it, by two intervening cultures.

Although our language contains many words of Latin derivation, most of them came to us with the Renaissance, through France and Italy. Only a handful of our Latin-derived words were bequeathed to us by the Romans themselves in our own land, and they are names of useful things which the Romans brought with them; *copper*, for instance, or *mint* (of money) or *street*. This last is the most significant: it was the roads which Rome brought that most affected the native inhabitants, who in awe, fear or gratitude, adopted the Latin word (*via*) *strata* into their native tongue as *street*. Six centuries later the Arabs, on their emergence from the roadless sands of the desert, did exactly the same thing, for the same reason, as the Arabic word *ṣirat* proclaims.

Britain took a long time to tame. Julius Caesar had twice invaded it, in 55 and 54 B.C., but only succeeded in securing the nominal submission of the tribes in the south-eastern corner. Julius was unable to follow up his enterprise, Augustus unwilling. Commerce became the surrogate for arms, and lucrative cargoes left British ports for Gaul and the Mediterranean: corn, cattle, gold, silver and iron, hides, slaves (so runs Strabo's catalogue) and, even in those days, highly intelligent dogs, the precursors of our modern sheep-dogs and fox-hounds. But across the Channel the legions watched, resentful and rapacious: one day this stubborn island must succumb to their unconquerable might. They had to wait for nearly a century: Caligula had assembled an army of invasion in the year 40, but, like those of two later megalomaniacs, it never got farther than Boulogne. Three years later Claudius, the new, elderly emperor who had succeeded his mad nephew, decided to conquer Britain. He knew that the occupation would be no walk-over, as had confidently been predicted. People had said that one legion, with a few auxiliaries, would be enough. Claudius took four, the IIIrd, Caesar's Own, from Strasbourg, the IXth, Spanish, from Austria, the XIVth, Twin, from Mainz, and the XXth, Victorious Valerian, from Neuss on the Lower Rhine. The campaign was a brilliant success. Claudius made a triumphal entry into Colchester, the capital of his principal opponent, while Vespasian, who was also to be emperor one day, directed the drive to the west. The formidable Caractacus, a cadet of the royal house of Colchester, escaped, and was for nine years, as a guerrilla leader, to harass the Romans. By the year 47, Rome was established from the Trent to the Severn, Colchester was refounded, and peopled with veterans. It became a colony, and the centre of the imperial cult, dedicated to the emperor Claudius. Gloucester and Lincoln received Roman foundations. The Mendip lead mines became Roman property, South Wales was assaulted and Caractacus, after his final defeat, sought refuge with the queen of the Brigantes, a tribal confederation living in what is now England north of the Humber, who handed him over to the Romans in chains. In A.D. 59 both in Wales and in the north hostility seethed. The Roman governor, Paulinus, had had experience in quelling revolts in the Atlas mountains, where he had learned to humble the elusive hillmen by cutting their line of supply with the plains. He now applied similar tactics to the Welsh: he decided to occupy the island of Anglesey, which was both a supply-base for the mountaineers and the headquarters of the Druids, whose addiction to human sacrifice shocked the Romans, particularly when the victims happened to be Roman prisoners. The expedition succeeded, the island was occupied, the Druids suppressed and their sacred groves felled.

Before Paulinus could exploit his victory, another revolt claimed his attention. The famous Boadicea now enters the story: it was humiliating for the Romans that in Britain, always in the forefront of feminism, so many of their opponents should have been women. Boadicea, the widow of an East Anglian Chieftain, had good reason to resent Roman domination. Her property had been confiscated to the treasury, her daughters had been raped and she had been scourged. She found ready allies in the tribe to her south, around Colchester, who saw themselves expropriated to provide land for the veterans, and taxed to maintain the exacting liturgies of the imperial cult. Boadicea and her horde swept down upon Colchester, destroyed the Claudian temple— the equivalent of burning down Government House—butchered the inhabitants, with the exception of those reserved for sacrifice in the tribal groves. London and St. Albans were abandoned to the insurgents. In the end Paulinus defeated Boadicea; but she left an abiding impression on the Roman imagination, so much so that Dio Cassius, writing a century and a half later, builds her up as a heroine of compelling eloquence. To the British, this first destruction of their capital by the forces of barbarism has always made a strong emotional appeal; and Boadicea has her memorial in the chivalrous lines of Lord Tennyson, no less than in the bronze quadriga at Westminster which, if it were in motion, would carry her headlong into the House of Commons.

Despite Boadicea's defeat, the Brigantes turned on the Romans within ten years. The fact was, the Britons were not interested in civilisation. Unlike the Gauls and the Spaniards, they never took the trouble to become Latin, and they never, except for a few quislings, tried to ape the Romans. Nevertheless, they could not be left to run riot as they wished, not by Rome. Fortunately for Rome, there came to Britain at this point a very remarkable man, and fortunately for us he was the father-in-law of the historian Tacitus, who has left us a charming little biography of him. His name was Agricola. He was a brilliant soldier; he tranquillized the Brigantes, and consolidated the occupation of Wales; he advanced into Scotland, whose inhabitants were ruder even than those of Yorkshire, and actually established a fort, now Inchtuthill, on the northern bank of the Tay. But Agricola was more than a great soldier: he was, as great soldiers of a later empire were so often to prove themselves, a wise and clement administrator. In a sentence Tacitus sums up this quality: "Such was his tact, that he made it appear that he had found men loyal, not made them so."

84

The conquest of Britain, the final subjugation (as it seemed) of this stubborn people, made a deep impression in Rome. The old Roman spirit still lived, said the proud Romans: an emperor, and an emperor to be, had once again led the legions to a victory which had been consolidated and extended by Roman arms and Roman wisdom. Tacitus' book must have had a wide public. A contemporary of Tacitus, the Jewish historian Josephus, makes both Agrippa II and the emperor Titus, when appealing to the Jews of Jerusalem to abandon a vain and hopeless struggle, cite Britain as an example of a land which thought itself safe from Roman arms, but had at last succumbed to them. To many a Roman, Britain was now the brightest jewel in the imperial crown.

But the battle of Britain was by no means yet won. A jealous Domitian withdrew Agricola at the height of his beneficent career. The forts were multiplied and strengthened, stone walls replaced turf ramparts, but still the sullen Britons refused to co-operate. The climax came in the year of Hadrian's accession, A.D. 117, when once again the northern Britons rose against their invaders. They wiped out a whole legion, the IXth Spanish, named after Hadrian's own countrymen: it was not a happy augury for the new reign.

That is why Hadrian now made his way to Britain: these restless, unreasonable Britons must be brought under control. Hadrian had known about the Britons from his childhood, because it was from his native province (as surviving jar-handles attest) that the uncouth islanders had imported their olive oil. So ardent a huntsman had probably heard about the famous British hounds; he may also have heard about the oysters which gave Tacitus an opportunity of sneering at Britons and Romans in the same sentence: they bred small pearls of a poor colour and not fit for export, he had heard, and he preferred to believe it because it was more likely that nature was deficient than that Roman greed was.

In Britain, as in many another province, the arrival of the emperor Hadrian was the stimulus of development and progress. It is from this event that the expansion of London dates. During the twenties of the second century it was ravaged by a fire, but when it was rebuilt, it came to enclose no less than 325 acres, which made it one of the largest Roman cities north of the Alps.

Many other cities were rebuilt, but, as Professor Richmond notes, they tended to reduce their compass, not extend it. Silchester, Canterbury, Chichester, Winchester, Leicester, Exeter all settled down to an area of about a hundred acres, smaller, by a quarter, than Hadrian's native Hispalis. Cirencester, St. Albans and Wroxeter were larger; but they were exceptions. For this contraction, two reasons may be assigned. The first is that, with the spread of security, it was no longer necessary to plan for an influx of refugees in times of trouble. The second, equally cogent, reason is that the Britons of those days, as of later centuries, were countrymen, not townsmen. In Italy, and other Latin countries, it has always been the towns that are the centres of civilisation, in England the country-houses. Britons have always cared more for the country than for the town, as the beauty of their gardens and the drabness of their cities still proves. The more the countryside flourished, the fewer Britons would wish to live in a town. "So, after completing his thorough-going military reforms, he set out for Britain. Here he found a great many things that needed putting to rights. He also built a wall, eighty miles long—he was the first to do it—to separate the Romans from the savages." Thus does Hadrian's biographer describe the emperor's achievements in Britain. Having "put things to rights", and so stabilized communications and urban development, both of which would mean increased revenue for Rome, Hadrian saw that, on one condition, Britain could be a useful source of something as valuable as money, and that was manpower. That condition was the protection of the one, short frontier. Most of the lands in which he had served, Germany, Austria, Syria, had long land frontiers, to protect which large numbers of troops were needed. Britain, being an island, had no such trouble. Once protect her from the northern savages, and her sons could fare forth to fight in any part of the world—as they have been doing ever since. From his experience on the Rhine-Danube frontier Hadrian knew, as the builders of later defensive systems were to discover, that to retire into a strong fortress was fatal. It deprives the defenders of the initiative, and in war, as in politics, to lose the initiative is the first step towards defeat. The Crusaders were to find this, the Knights of Rhodes and of Malta were to find it, the builders of the Maginot Line were to find it. Hadrian had a far more modern outlook. He knew, as the British army in the Egyptian desert were to demonstrate in 1940, that a force on the strategic defensive (as the Romans were in the face of the northern barbarians) must continually adopt the tactical offensive. The use of a line of static forts, he realised, was small. What was needed was a system of fortifications which would give his army the maximum mobility, would ensure that it would always have the initiative, and would give it control over a wide area and the vital communications which furnished the supplies of that area. And so he built his wall from the Tyne to the Solway.

It is easy to form a wrong impression of the nature and function of the wall. It was never intended to be, and never was, a rigid continuous barrier, to seal up and stop any movement between its two sides. It had a double function: to *control movement* by the inhabitants of the country on the north-south axis, and to *accelerate movement* by the security forces along the east-west axis. The whole strategy of the wall was conceived in terms of *movement*. The wall was really a triple system of defence. First there is the wall itself, then to the immediate south of it there is a double dyke or Vallum, and third south of that there is a road, running east and west. The Vallum consists of two great banks, with an open space of eighty feet between, and a flat-bottomed ditch, twenty feet wide and ten deep, in the middle. This vallum was made after forts on the wall were built, as we can see by the fact that it swerves from the straight line in order to skirt the forts on the south. Between the south bank of the vallum and the ditch there was a covered way, or patrol track, connected with the milecastles of the wall by means of causeways over the ditch and gaps in the north bank of the vallum. Thus the vallum could be continually policed. It marked the southern limit of the military zone, from which, as from modern "W.D. areas", the public were excluded: they could cross the vallum only at the forts, under the eyes of the guards.

The wall was originally planned to run from Pons Aelius (the new bridge over the Tyne which bore the same name as that which was to lead to Hadrian's mausoleum in Rome), or Newcastle, to a point on the Solway, Bowness, below which the estuary cannot be forded. While the work was in progress, so effective had it already become that the eastern end of the wall had to be extended to Wallsend (to which it gave its name) in order to stop smuggling. The total length of the whole wall is thus eighty Roman or seventy-three English miles. The wall is magnificently sited. It runs along the high ground to the north of the Tyne and Irthing rivers, and commands an uninterrupted view of many miles to north and south alike. Its average altitude is five hundred feet, but at Whinshields it rises to one thousand two hundred and thirty. The design appears to have been altered during the construction, as the barrier is not of uniform dimensions throughout its length. The eastern forty-five miles consist of a rampart of stone, originally ten Roman feet wide at the base later reduced to eight, sixteen feet high to the platform, and, allowing for a breastwork and crenellations, twenty feet high in all. The western section of the wall was originally of less robust construction, because in that region limestone, which produced the lime necessary for grouting, is not found. From the Irthing to Bowness the rampart was of turf, twenty Roman feet wide, carrying milecastles or fortlets of turf and timber and turrets of stone, two between each pair of milecastles. On the north side, there was a ditch, twenty-seven feet wide on the average, and nine deep, except where the wall stands above the cliffs of the Great Whin Sill.

When, in the eastern section, the 8-foot stone wall replaced the 10-foot one, the turf wall of the western section, for about four miles west of the Irthing, was replaced by an 8-foot stone wall, which for the first two miles took a course slightly to the north of the turf wall. Finally, about A.D. 160, the rest of the western section of the wall, as far as Bowness, was replaced by a 9-foot stone wall.

The wall was built by legionaries and other troops in sectors of forty to fifty feet long. As each unit completed its stint, it inscribed its mark at each end of the sector. Sometimes a whole legion is recorded by number, or by its emblem, the boar of the XXth, for instance; more frequently a detachment inscribed the name of the centurion in charge. The masonry is ashlar, bonded with a mortar made of sand, lime and blood, facing a rubble core. The stones are small, seldom as much as a foot square, more often eight inches by nine. This seems curiously un-Roman, until we reflect that the whole work was done by hand, without the aid of ropes and pulleys, and that every stone had to be carried to the site on the back of man or beast, from quarries seven or eight miles off in Cumberland. Allowance is made for the English climate: every five metres a drain runs under the wall, to allow the rain and snow to feed the ditch on the north side.

Through the ages, the wall has diminished in height. The Venerable Bede says that in his day it was twelve feet broad and twenty-one feet high in some places: Camden, in the sixteenth century, gives the height as fifteen. Today, it is still eight feet high in places, and the builders' inscriptions, reminiscent of those attached by British troops to their public works during the last war, may still be read *in situ*.

The wall was manned by a garrison stationed in no less than seventeen forts, disposed at four-mile intervals (see map on page 79). At every mile there was a fortlet, or milecastle, with two signal-turrets between each pair. The forts were laid out on the usual Roman plan, and many of them can still be studied in sufficient detail to enable us to imagine them as they were, with the headquarters, the barracks, the orderly-room, the baths, the latrines (then, as now, rough replicas of the more refined civilian plumbing), the stores for corn and oil. The corn was ground either by hand or at one of three water-mills of which traces have been found. The local coal was used by some units. Outside the forts are sometimes to be seen the relics of the *vici* or suburbs occupied by camp-followers, sutlers and the like.

The wall was intended partly as an intelligence network; and such was its efficiency that a message could be flashed from one coast to the other in a matter of minutes. Out came the troops, and by the time the enemy had plodded on to within reach of the wall they would be surrounded, outflanked and overwhelmed. There were plenty of gates in the wall, for the passage of innocent wayfarers and merchants, and also to allow the troops to dart out into the open at whatever point was tactically most advantageous.

It is easy to become sentimental about the wall, to imagine solitary legionaries standing in Leighton-like poses on the lonely rampart, dreaming of Rome. In fact, they were not legionaries, and they had never even seen Rome, most of them. There were, it is true, three legions permanently stationed in Britain, at York, Chester and Caerleon; but these legions were composed chiefly of Gauls, Germans and Spaniards. The wall was a frontier, and as such was manned by a frontier force, which like all frontier forces was recruited from peripheral tribes, men from Belgium or Hungary, for instance.

The real impact of the wall on a present day visitor is far from being sentimental. It impresses by its amazing modernity, by its on-the-toes conception of strategy. It is impossible to contemplate it or any portion of it without seeing men in motion, sweeping over those wide moors, to the north and the south, into those gaunt, blue distances, clattering across the silent fells, hushing the sheep and the curlews, concentrating inexorably to vanquish and overcome all their enemies. Hadrian's wall, even in decay (and it has provided the stones for more pacific walls over an area of many square miles besides being used by General Wade as a quarry for his military road), is the most romantic surviving memorial, not only to the *Pax Romana* but to the emperor Hadrian; and it is in England.

Chapter XI

FAREWELL TO THE WEST

WHILE he was in Britain, Hadrian received some bad news. It came from Egypt. Alexandria might be a centre of learning, but it was also a city notorious for riots. In those days, as in ours, an Egyptian mob was one of the most turbulent and destructive to be found anywhere. On this occasion, it was not a man who had excited them but a beast. Apis had appeared again. This was the sacred bullock, which, so Herodotus had been told, was begotten by a shaft of light from heaven. It could be recognised by certain markings, which included representations of the sun and moon. The appearance of a new Apis naturally led to great rejoicing. It also led to much dispute, as to where the animal should be kept, and who should have the right of looking after so lucrative a creature. That was what the Alexandrians were rioting about. Hadrian had no wish to go to Egypt at that particular time: he still had work to do in Gaul and Spain. So he wrote a stern letter to the Alexandrians, and that had its effect. But Hadrian knew that one day he would have to visit Egypt.

The winter of 121 was spent in Provence. This region had been Roman for many years, and had been Greek before that. Hadrian founded a new colony, what is now Avignon. He went to Nîmes, and here more bad news reached him. Plotina was dead. The only woman Hadrian ever loved had left him. His wife, Sabina, he detested: she returned his hate; she boasted that she had ensured that she would never bear children to such a monster. But they stuck to each other. For Hadrian, a wife was a respectable convention; Sabina enjoyed being empress—and Hadrian, as we have seen, insisted that she should be treated as one. But there was no sentiment on either side. Plotina was altogether different. It was Plotina who had made Hadrian, Plotina who had brought him into Trajan's family, Plotina who had encouraged the susceptible emperor to cherish and promote his handsome nephew, Plotina who, at Trajan's death, had made certain that Hadrian should succeed. She had done her work well, and now she was gone.

Hadrian composed memorial hymns to her and wore black for nine days. He used to say that although she had asked much of him, he had never once refused her requests—so wise, so modest had they been. Hadrian commemorated her there in Nîmes, with a splendid temple. This is not the famous *Maison Carrée*, which had been standing for more than a century, and it is no longer possible to identify the memorial of this great and good woman, who exerted a larger and more beneficent influence on the destinies of Rome than any other of whom we have record.

In the neighbouring town of Apt, Hadrian placed a memorial of a different kind, but one which is very revealing. Hadrian loved his horses. His favourite hunter was called Borysthenes, and he evidently had for him the same sort of affection as Wellington was to have for Copenhagen. Borysthenes died at Apt, so Hadrian placed him in a fine tomb, and on it he had carved a horsey little poem he had composed himself. It says:

> "Borysthenes the Alan
> Caesar's hunter
> Over plain and marsh
> And the mounds of Tuscany
> Went like the wind.
> After the boars of Hungary
> He chased, and no boar
> Dared wound him with its glistening tushes,
> Nor did any saliva
> Ever touch his tail's tip
> As generally happens;
> But in the flower of his youth,
> Sound in wind and limb,
> He lived out his day
> And now he lies here."

It is a pleasant picture, the imperial patron and poetaster, embellishing this province which was to become the *Provence* par excellence, erecting temples and memorials, and proving to the inhabitants that the new empire was indeed the "best state of citizenship", even as Augustus had claimed it would be, and perambulating the lovely countryside that was in a later century to breed Daudet and Cézanne.

After this busy and productive sojourn in the south of France,

Hadrian moved on to Spain. But not to his native Andalusia. He spent the winter of 122-3 in the romantic seaside citadel of Tarraco, the modern Tarragona, where, with his usual anti-quarian piety, he restored the temple of Augustus at his own expense. But this bounty was of no avail in the difficult negotiations which Hadrian had now to undertake. In Roman times, as in our own, the inhabitants of northern Africa had as strong a zeal for independence as any peoples in or near the Roman orbit. They were almost as tiresome as the Britons. The three countries that we now call Tunisia, Algeria and Morocco formed three provinces. Tunisia was called *Africa*—only to it was the name applied, just as to a Roman *Asia* always meant the province between the Dardanelles and Rhodes. Then, to the west, there was *Numidia*, and finally the twin provinces of *Mauretania*, the eastern called *Caesariensis* (which through the Arabic *Al-Jezaïr* has given us Algeria), and finally the western called *Tingitana* from *Tingis*, its northern port, which is today *Tangier*. It was in Mauretania that the frontier of Spain really lay, just as at one epoch it was said that Britain's was on the Rhine, and for the same reason. Again and again the ferocious tribesmen of north Africa were to shew that they were only too eager to loot the prosperous lands across the water. Augustus had planted a number of military colonies in the province, both inside and outside the Pillars of Hercules, as the Straits of Gibraltar were called. Hadrian was determined that here, as elsewhere in the empire, the new frontier policy must be put into force. But where were the troops to come from, because if a thorough pacification were to be attempted it would be a matter of many columns? Hadrian called a conference of delegates from all over Spain. He explained his plan, and shewed the inhabitants that it was their concern as much as anyone's that the nether shore of the Mediterranean, whose bastions the dwellers in the southern Baetica daily beheld, should be pacified. The delegates turned the plan down flat. The Spanish would have nothing to do with it: although it was their own legion, the IXth, Spanish, which had so recently been annihilated, they pointed out that Trajan had expressly forbidden the levying of troops in Spain, which had already been im-poverished by the praetor. The "Italians" were kinder, and brushed the request aside "with a joke"—after all Hadrian was one of them, and they were very proud of him. So Hadrian, for the moment, turned again to the embellishment of Spain. Up went the temples, through went the roads, and a grateful people erected statue after statue of their benefactor, and had them gilded, by a special artist brought all the way from Carthage, for the Phoenicians had always been more apt at so garish a finish than the plain-mannered Romans.

One day, as Hadrian was walking about in a garden at Tarraco, a slave, one of his host's, set upon him with a sword. Fortunately Hadrian was very strong, and easily disarmed the man. When the terrified servants ran up, Hadrian handed him over to them. Clearly, the poor fellow must be mad, and so it was to the doctors, and not to the gaolers, that Hadrian ordered him to be committed. He himself was quite unruffled by the whole affair. His conduct made the most favourable impression. In our own days it is an axiom that anyone who assaults a member of the Royal Family is insane: it is interesting to read of this Hadrianic precedent for it.

Hadrian had by no means abandoned his Mauretanian expedition. Apart from strategic considerations, no emperor, nor the son of an emperor, had ever set foot in the country. That was a powerful lure with Hadrian. There was also the Garden of the Hesperides, that lay just south of Tingis; and, in more recent times, there had been that learned king Juba, who had written such absorbing histories, and had married Cleopatra's daughter. It would be interesting, too, to see the originals of those strange and uncouth figures that he had laughed at in the mosaics of Italica when he was a boy. And his friend Turbo had told him so much about the country and its people,—he must visit Mauretania. So to Mauretania he went, and successfully finished Turbo's work. This is all the more remarkable, because a north African war is normally a long war. The Romans discovered that, just as the French and Spanish were later to do. Hadrian's campaign was a bright exception. The results of it can be descried in the ruins of Volubilis, the lovely Roman town not far from Fez, perched on a rounded hill, and embowered in olive trees. By the third century it was a large and flourishing city, and the thirty oil-presses which still stand within its walls attest its felicity. And yet, as Hadrian was to discover to his cost, in a far more serious context, the Semitic character is tough and enduring. Not even he could make Mauretania Roman. In Volubilis there are many of the standard Roman themes to be found in the mosaics—

Flora and the Seasons, Hercules, Orpheus. But it is the animals of Africa that predominate—the lion, the elephant, the panther, with many and various fish, including the langouste. In the museum at Rabat there are two bronzes from Volubilis. Both are exquisite, with an almost Hadrianic grace, but both represent local subjects: one is a horse, the other a Berber. Rome was still a foreigner here.

From Mauretania Hadrian returned to Spain, and soon sailed away to Ephesus. North Africa was to see him again: but he never went back to the western provinces.

Chapter XII

MORNINGLAND

EPHESUS! It was one of Hadrian's favourite cities. It was the capital of Asia, the richest market west of the Taurus, a city of schools, temples and sumptuous buildings. He knew it from the old days, when he had been in the east with Trajan. And quite recently he had had dealings with it. The elders' association had appealed to him direct in the matter of the refusal of the heirs of certain deceased members to pay up the arrears due to that body. Hadrian, like the good administrator he was, had replied that he would refer the matter to the governor, who would see that justice was done. And now here he was in person, the first ruling emperor since Augustus to cross the Aegean on a peaceful errand, the first, except for Nero on his Greek tour, to leave Italy for other ends than war or conquest. It was indeed a new departure.

And for Hadrian what a solace to be back again within the radiance of Hellenism. This land was so antique, so rich in myth, in history. Monuments from the days of old stood in its cities, many of them eloquent of other, mysterious races, the demiurges of mankind, who had laboured to fashion the fabric of the world, so that at last the Greeks might inhabit and illuminate it. That was the Anatolia, the Land of Morning, to which the artist emperor had come. But he had come on business. It is all too easy to picture Hadrian, the philosopher king, strolling through the empire, discussing the arts, putting up temples and monuments, and being hailed as a god in return. In fact, Hadrian was out primarily, here as elsewhere, to overhaul the administration. The proof of this intention is that in the two years, 124 and 125, which he spent in what is now Turkey, he confined his travels to the two provinces of Asia and Bithynia. Earthquakes, to which the region is disastrously liable, had recently brought ruin to a number of cities, and this must be repaired. But in the more ardent atmosphere of the Levant Hadrian found it impossible to maintain his rule of never associating his own name with what he presented or built. The people simply insisted on it. To the citizens of Asia,

Athens. The remnant of the Olympieum as it now appears, from the east, with the Acropolis in the background (page 102).

Hadrian's Arch. A corner of the Acropolis is just visible above the right-hand pier. This gateway divided the old and new cities. On the side furthest from us it bears the inscription "This is the city of Theseus the former city", and on that nearest to us "This is of Hadrian and not the city of Theseus". Whether it was Hadrian, who preferred to give credit to earlier builders rather than to himself, or a grateful Athens who thus inscribed the Gate, we do not know (page 103).

Rome. The Temple of Venus and Rome, from the Colosseum. The controversial podium is seen in the foreground. The clipped circular bushes mark the positions of the pillars. Behind the *cella* and the apse an exactly similar *cella* and apse were placed symmetrically back to back, the colonnade surrounding the whole structure. (See Figure 1, page 110) On the left is the Arch

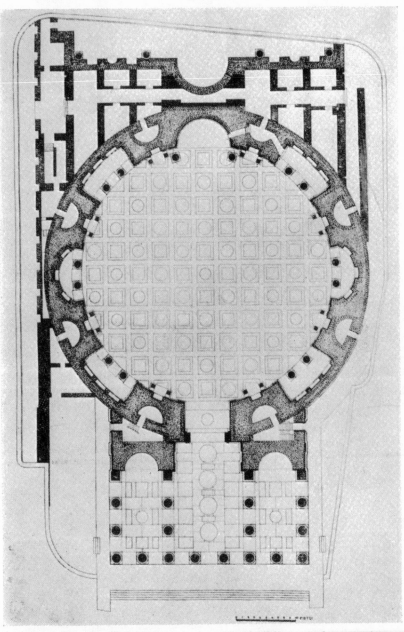

Rome. The Pantheon, ground plan. The buildings at the opposite end of the rotunda to the porch formed part of the adjacent Baths of Agrippa. The height of the rotunda is exactly the same as its diameter, 43·30 metres. (See Figure 3, page 114)

Rome. The Pantheon
from the north.

it was easy and natural to regard him as the embodiment of Fortune, of Dionysus its bringer, indeed of Zeus himself. Their imaginations ran on such lines, they liked gods to be familiar, and personal. Paul the apostle had been hailed as a god; and in Ephesus itself, whose inhabitants were convinced that their famous statue of Artemis had come to them from the very hand of Zeus, the citizens had taken handkerchiefs to be touched by Paul, and then used them for the healing of the sick. Witchcraft and quackery, the "curious arts" of Acts xix, 19, flourished, as they always do when faith has over-ripened into credulity. But faith was there, too; and it was but natural for it to find its focus in the greatest of mankind. So, when at Cyzicus, the citizens, in gratitude for Hadrian's earthquake relief measures, decided to erect a temple which should be, and became, one of the Seven Wonders of the World, Hadrian not only accepted the dedication of the temple, but contributed towards the cost of it from his own purse. And there was to be an annual festival called by his name, too.

A number of new cities were founded which bore Hadrian's name; they were called Hadrianopolis, but it is good to record that one was called Hadrianotherae, which means Hadrian's Hunts, from the splendid runs he had enjoyed in its vicinity.

One of Hadrian's economic measures was to increase the coinage of Asia, to put more money into circulation. Formerly the mint had been at Pergamum. Augustus had transferred it to Ephesus, but Pergamum had regained it under Nerva. Hadrian now gave the right of minting coins to at least ten cities in Asia. The ancient deities appeared on these coins, Artemis for Ephesus, Asklepios for Pergamum, and so on. This was no mere piece of antiquarianism: it stressed the individuality of the venerable cities of Asia in the new Hadrianic unity of empire.

On his way north—for it was in Bithynia that the year 124 was passed—Hadrian paid a visit to Troy. Here he was shewn a monument that purported to be the tomb of Ajax. It was in ruins. Hadrian at once gave orders for its restoration, as he was to do for the tombs of other heroes of the past. It was the sort of thing that appealed to his romantic mind. "*Data sunt ipsis quoque fata sepulcris,*" Juvenal had written—"Even to a tomb, Comes its inevitable doom." Hadrian could reverse it.

The ultimate goal of Hadrian's Bithynian travels was Trapezus, or Trebizond, the name, which means *table*, being taken from the little tableland above the port on which the old town stood, and still stands. It is a beautiful town, with its acropolis flanked by two great chasms, the southern outpost of the glowering Caucasus. It was an ancient Greek colony and trading-post. In more recent times it had become one of the chief bases of a Roman fleet; and the Black Sea, ever since Pompey had chased King Mithradates all the way to the Crimea, nearly two hundred years earlier, was a Roman lake. Bithynia had always been an uneasy province to govern, because, despite the affable charm of its inhabitants (which has lasted to our own day), they possessed that desire to annoy their rulers which so often accompanies it. Strictly speaking, Bithynia was a "senatorial" province, that is, one of the peaceful provinces which the senate was permitted to administer through governors appointed from its own ranks, known as proconsuls. But more than once Caesar had had to step in and send out a special *legatus* of his own. This had occurred both under Claudius and under Nero, and finally, in the year 111 Trajan had, by agreement with the senate, despatched to Bithynia one of the most famous of all colonial governors, the Younger Pliny, from whose letters we gain a more lively and intimate picture of Roman provincial administration than from any other source. All sorts of people made trouble, including the Christians, or, in reality, those who did not like them. Even the fire brigades might be a source of sedition. Pliny wanted to allow one of them to form a club. Trajan, who must have known the Levant better than his friend, replied that any such association would inevitably become a hotbed of politics. Hadrian, who after his inspection was in his turn to place the province under a special commissioner, was also, as usual, bent on improving its economic status. Trapezus was a great fishery centre, the principal catch being tunny. Hadrian therefore ordered the construction of a new harbour for the benefit of the fishermen. He also—a charming personal touch— placed on the roof of a prominent building in the harbour a large gilded copper fish, as though to encourage the others.

Trapezus was embellished with the usual statue of the emperor. It was not a good one, as we know by a curious literary chance. Shortly after his visit to Trapezus, Hadrian sent out as governor of Cappadocia one of his learned friends, Arrian, and bade him make the complete survey of the coast of the Black Sea that Hadrian had been unable to make. This Arrian did, and the book was published some six years later. While he was at Trapezus, from which his expedition was to start, Arrian wrote a letter to the emperor. After flattering Hadrian by saying that his return, via Trapezus, had given just the same satisfaction as that of Xenophon and his ten thousand in days gone by, he goes on: "The altars are already in position, but they are made of coarse stone, and so the inscription is not clearly carved. It looks like native work. I have had the altars replaced by new ones of white stone, and the inscription very finely cut. Your statue fits in well with the scheme—it looks out over the sea—but as far as the workmanship is concerned, it is neither like you, nor is it attractive. Please send a statue worthy of being called *yours*. The site is ideal for a lasting memorial of you." No doubt such letters often came in, from all over the empire, and the traffic in official statues and busts must have been heavy. The heads of two hundred and fifty of Hadrian have survived to this day.

It was in Bithynia that Hadrian formed his famous and fatal attachment to Antinoüs, a lad of whose origin nothing is known, except that he came from the city of Bithynion. This had changed its name to Claudiopolis. Hadrian restored the original name, just as he was later to do at Mantineia, and the grateful citizens to return the compliment adopted Hadrian's name as well. They also founded a festival called after Hadrian and Antinoüs jointly, from which it may be inferred that they were proud of the association. Antinoüs, at the time when Hadrian met him, must have been a lad of about eighteen. He was broad-shouldered and quite exceptionally handsome. Most of the busts of him that survive, and there are some five hundred of them, twice the number of Hadrian's, shew him in a posthumous idealisation. With Antinoüs melancholy enters Roman sculpture, but the Romans never succeeded in portraying godhead. Their deified emperors and Antinoüses are still human: it was only the Greeks who could express the divine in stone; just as in later days, western painters represented their Holy Families and saints in human guise, whereas the eastern eikon-painters and mosaicists, in their Almighty Fathers and All-holy Virgins, suggest tremendous and transcendental divinity. It is one of the cleavages between western and eastern thought. It seems probable, nevertheless, that the beautiful head of Antinoüs from Olympia (see Plate 20) shews him as he was, in life.

Of Antinoüs and the many statues of him Sir Kenneth Clark, in *The Nude* (John Murray) has this to say: "For almost the first time since the 4th century a type of beauty is taken from a real head and not from a copy-book . . . we feel once more, though remotely enough, the warmth of an individual achievement. . . . The physical character of Antinoüs is still perceptible when, after its long banishment, the Apollonian nude returns in the person of Donatello's David."

More than eighteen hundred years after his death, Antinoüs could still affect an English poet. Charles Tennyson, in his life of his Laureate grandfather, recalls that Edmund Gosse saw Lord Tennyson stop in front of a bust of Antinoüs in the British Museum and say "in his deep, slow voice: Ah—this is the inscrutable Bithynian. If we knew what he knew, we should understand the ancient world."

Whether the relations between the emperor Hadrian and his beautiful young favourite were carnal or not, we cannot be sure. But what we can be certain of is this: that for the next nine years Antinoüs was the emperor's inseparable companion, that many people did suppose that their association was based on a physical relationship, and that they did not reprobate it in the least, particularly in the Hellenic world in which Hadrian was most at home. However much we may deplore this fact, it simply is not possible to equate ancient and modern canons of morality. Of Antinoüs, his relations with Hadrian, his tragic end and posthumous renown, more will be said in Chapter XX.

Before recrossing the Aegean, the emperor made one more trip to the interior. Some two hundred miles east of Ephesus, up on the plateau, was a little town called Melissa. Here was the tomb of Alcibiades, the brilliant and erratic Athenian whom his countrymen condemned just when in their direst straits he might have saved them. He had been murdered here in Asia, while he was on his way to the court of the Persian king. As a boy, this drawling dandy—he could never pronounce his r's—had been famous for his beauty, and had been the darling of Socrates. Alcibiades-Antinoüs: his memory must be honoured. A statue of white Parian marble was placed upon his tomb, and an annual sacrifice ordained in his memory.

So at last, in the autumn of the year 125, Hadrian arrived in Athens, the city of his soul.

Chapter XIII

ATHENS

EUROPE owes its faith, arts and civilisation to three cities, Jerusalem, Athens and Rome. Hadrian influenced all three in a manner and to a degree that no other man has ever done, before or since. Jerusalem he disliked, Rome he mistrusted, Athens he adored. In Athens Hadrian saw the heart of his faith and philosophy. There, in that silver light, more genial even than that of Italy, above the glittering waves, shone the citadel of his being, the *iostephanoi Athenai*, the violet-crowned city, as Pindar had called it. Here Hadrian could indeed be a Hellene, and lead the good life of the philosopher. Or so he thought. In fact, Athens was not quite the city he imagined it to be. In outward aspect it had not altered very much from the days of Pericles. There stood the Acropolis, with its twin temples, full of life and joy, there down below was the so-called Theseum, "faultily faultless, icily regular, splendidly null", as though to give point to the inexplicable perfection of the buildings above. The Agora was the same, and the great theatre of Dionysus, which had seen so many famous "firsts". But a closer view shewed a very different picture. Ever since, two centuries before, Sulla had sacked Athens, the city had been in decline. During the Roman civil wars she was subject to extortions from both sides, and unfortunately ended up on the side of Antony, which turned out to be the wrong one. The victorious Augustus did not care for Athens. Its trade languished, while its rival Corinth flourished. The general mass of the citizens were terribly poor, so poor that when, during Hadrian's reign, the price of bread rose very slightly above the normal, the people wanted to stone the distinguished man who was in charge of the market. But, just as in our own day, among the poverty-stricken Athenians there were men of fabulous wealth, such as Hipparchus, whose grandson, Herodes Atticus, was to be the Onassis of his age.

The looting of the city did not end with the official sack under Sulla. Greek antiquities became the fashion in Rome. Sulla had started the vogue when he ordered columns taken from Athens to be used in the repair of the Roman capitol. At least one of the ships that he had crammed with works of art sank after rounding Cape Malea. Another ship, loaded with columns, sank off Tunis, whither it had probably been blown by a storm. Twenty years later the traffic was in full swing: Cicero writes to his friend Atticus: "I was glad to learn that you had bought me some statues in Pentelic marble; send me them as soon as you can, I want them at once", and "I have received the statue in Megara marble that you sent me. If you find any other suitable pieces don't hesitate to buy them for me." Cicero at least paid for what he took. But others were less nice. The bronze cornices, with heads of Dionysus and Ariadne, were wrenched from the arsenal at Piraeus, and they, too, went west. Caligula and Nero both carried off what they fancied. Another batch of fine bronzes of various ages was found in Piraeus in 1959, the warehouse in which they were stored having collapsed before they could be shipped.

But there was still plenty to see at Athens. The Elder Pliny reckoned that there were about 3,000 statues in Athens, Delphi and Olympia, adding the very un-German comment—"who could count them, and what good would it be?" The city had, in fact, become a sort of Williamsburg. Pausanias, who wrote his guide-book just after Hadrian's time, gives a long list of tourist attractions, and mentions frequently the guides who would shew visitors round. Roman taste was not good. Pliny's favourite statue was one of a dog licking its wounds. Pausanias, knowing his public, particularly recommends one with fingernails of real silver.

Such was the city and the society to which Hadrian came in the year 125. He decided at once on a large programme of rehabilitation. First, the city needed replanning. During the troubled centuries a number of squalid buildings had been huddled together for protection under the walls of the Acropolis. They could not be displaced without causing great hardship, and yet decent housing and modern amenities must be provided. Hadrian solved this problem in exactly the same way as Marshal Lyautey was to solve it at Rabat and other Moroccan cities. The old was to be left untouched, and the new laid out as a faubourg, but on a completely new scale. For the centre of his new Athens, Hadrian chose the Temple of Zeus Olympios. This grandiose conception had been started by Antiochus Epiphanes in 174 B.C. It had never been finished. Its completion would make a big impression, would give a central feature to Hadrian's new town, and not least of all, would endorse his own right to be called Olympian. So the work was started. The next thing the city needed was a decent water supply. Hadrian brought it from Kephissia in an aqueduct which supplied the city until the second decade of the twentieth century, when the so-called Marathon dam was completed.

The new town stretched as far as the slopes of Mount Hymettus. It contained Temples of Hera (with whom the empress Sabina had been flatteringly assimilated) and of Panhellenic Zeus, to be the centre of Hadrian's new Panhellenic league. A Pantheon contained records of the emperor's good deeds, the old portico of Caesar and Augustus—it, too, is still there—formed the city's western limit, and a triumphal gate its southern (see Plate 9). Just to the east of the old fifth century agora, Hadrian built a library of which vestiges remain.

While these works were going forward Hadrian was taking steps to restore Athenian finances by increasing her taxable territory and by direct subsidies. He ensured that despite the lucrative demands of the export market the gymnasium of Athens should be adequately supplied with olive oil for the use of the athletes. And he found plenty of time to talk with learned men. Some of his conversations have come down to us. The most remarkable record is the most trivial. It consists of so-called dialogues, with Secundus and Epictetus, which are no more than infantile question-and-answer, such as, "What is death? What everyone flees from and no one escapes", or "What is harder than iron? The heart of the proud." The interest of this exercise lies in the fact that it is the origin of all later question-and-answer lesson books. As early as the seventh century it was making its way into such languages as Arabic and Armenian. It even reached Iceland. A pupil of Duns Scotus took the Dialogues to Oxford in the fourteenth century. The Church catechism, and many another manual, adopted their style. The Dialogues can be traced back to the third century, and it is quite probable that they did embody recollections of what someone's grandfather remembered over-hearing when he was a boy, and Hadrian was in Athens.

A more solid testimony to Hadrian's philosophic attainments is provided by Philostratus, who wrote his *Lives of the Sophists* about two generations after Hadrian's death. There was, for instance, Dionysius of Miletus. Hadrian appointed him a governor as he appointed Arrian, enrolled him as a knight, and made him a member of the Alexandria Museum, an international academy, whose distinguished fellows were given free maintenance.

Another friend was Polemo. He had met Hadrian in Asia, and had captivated him at once, so completely that he persuaded the emperor to abandon his plan of founding Olympic Games at Ephesus, and to found them at Smyrna instead. Hadrian also provided funds for the building of a corn-market, a gymnasium and a splendid temple—all due to Polemo. The sophist already enjoyed the privilege of free travel in official post-vehicles. Hadrian made it hereditary in perpetuity. Polemo, too, was elected to the Museum, and given a nice present of about ten thousand pounds into the bargain. Hadrian would not hear a word against him. When the people of Smyrna complained that he had been helping himself to public money, Hadrian merely wrote to him saying, "Please render me an account of the money *I gave you*"—which Polemo no doubt had much pleasure in shewing to the people of Smyrna. The most charming anecdote about Polemo and his hold on Hadrian concerns the latter days of his reign, but may be told here. Antoninus (whom Hadrian had adopted) was governor of Asia, and one day he arrived in Smyrna unannounced. Polemo was away, but Antoninus commandeered his house, being the best in the town. When Polemo got back late at night, he found himself kept out of his own house by the Roman guards. He was furious, and there and then turned Antoninus out. Caesar's heir, and governor as well, naturally sent off a despatch to Rome, complaining of the insult. Hadrian saw that both sides had been in the wrong. How could he settle it without rebuking either? He did so want the two to be friends when he was gone. What Hadrian did was this: in his will, by which the empire devolved on Antoninus, he wrote: "It was Polemo who persuaded me to do this." The two men became firm friends, and often used to make jokes about the incident. One day Polemo arrived in Rome and went to see Antoninus. The emperor was delighted. Turning to a member of his staff he said: "See that Polemo is given a good, comfortable house to stay in— and see that no one turns him out of it, either." On another occasion Polemo had been judging a dramatic performance and had dismissed one of the actors, who was so bad that the sensitive Polemo could not bear to listen to him. The actor went off to complain to the emperor. "Polemo told me to clear out, Lord Caesar," said the indignant actor. "When did he do that?" asked the emperor. "Almost as soon as I had begun, Lord Caesar, in the early afternoon!" "You are lucky," said Antoninus, "he turned me out at midnight."

The same sort of *Arabian Nights* atmosphere surrounds Hadrian's relations with Favorinus, an extremely eminent man of letters. He came from Arles, in the south of France. His favourite language was Greek, which he spoke with such grace that it was impossible, so his pupil Aulus Gellius says, to render the nuances of his discourse in Latin, the language in which Aulus himself wrote. Favorinus, like a modern "publicist", was prepared to scatter his wisdom broadcast: he would lay down the law about Plato's style, give advice to nursing mothers, conduct a mock Socratic dialogue to humble a youth who was shewing off, utter a creaking witticism to a silly young pedant who was fond of old-fashioned words, which he said the lad only used to prevent people knowing what he was saying: why not go one better, and say nothing at all? Once when Hadrian and he had been arguing about whether a certain word was used by reputable authors, Favorinus gave in, though the company knew he was right. When they chid him for it, Favorinus answered: "You're quite wrong, dear boys: allow me to believe that the wisest man on earth is the one who has thirty legions."

Favorinus was nominated high priest, whereupon Hadrian decided to have a little joke with him. He knew that being a priest of any sort was not much in Favorinus' line, and was amused to see how Favorinus would get out of it. The eminent sophist stood up before the assembled fathers and pleaded that in accordance with the established laws of Athens he was exempt from public service "because he was a philosopher". At this Hadrian pretended to be outraged—Favorinus a *philosopher*? Rubbish! the emperor would vote against him, whereupon Favorinus, seeing which way the wind was blowing, cut in: "O my King, I've had a dream I must tell you about. My teacher Dion appeared to me, and, in respect of this very matter, charged and reminded me that we are sent into this world not only for ourselves but for our fatherland. I obey my teacher: I undertake the job." Hadrian, who enjoyed this sort of fun, had taken the whole thing as a joke, and so, obviously, had Favorinus; but the literal-minded and obsequious aldermen thought that Hadrian was really annoyed with Favorinus, so they solemnly went in a body and pulled down his statue. When Favorinus heard about it he laughed, and said: "At any rate, I've come off better than Socrates." Favorinus came from Gaul, and there is a Gallic spice about his best-known remark. He used to say that there were three paradoxes in his life: he was a Gaul who lived as a Hellene, he was a eunuch who had been accused of adultery with a consul's wife, he had contradicted Caesar and was still alive.

Life with such men as Favorinus and Polemo may well have been amusing; and it is pleasant to think of Hadrian relaxing in such society after his administrative drudgery. But the stories have their sad side. They shew that Athens, which Hadrian reverenced as the source of all light, was little more than a tarnished mirror, its philosophy clever chat, its citizens indigent sycophants. The sun of Hellenism had set: all Hadrian saw was its twilight.

Chapter XIV

HADRIAN'S ROME

IT was not only Athens that received the emperor's bounty, for not only Athens had been left desolate and oppressed by earlier Roman masters. A friend of Cicero's, in a famous letter, had described to him the melancholy spectacle which greeted the eye of the traveller as he coasted along the Grecian shore and beheld so many famous cities in ruins. Much of the damage had been repaired, and Corinth was once again a flourishing city, though even Corinth was in need of an aqueduct, which Hadrian was delighted to supply. To others he gave roads, baths, temples, the usual gifts: to catalogue them all would turn a biography into a Baedeker. At Mantineia, once again, besides restoring the ancient name, he honoured an ancient hero, Epameinondas, the Theban general, whose grave he restored. In the summer of 126 he set sail for the west. He called at Delphi, and exchanged vapid question and answer (about Homer's parentage) with the resident sybil. He broke his journey in Sicily, attracted, no doubt, by its imposing and romantic Greek memorials, the temples of Agrigentum and Segesta, by Syracuse with its theatres, temple, now the cathedral, to-day the only Doric temple still used as a place of worship, the Spring of Arethusa, and the memories of two famous sieges, the former by the Athenians, which had ended in disaster, the latter by the Romans, in which Archimedes had met his death. The emperor also climbed up Mount Etna, eleven thousand feet high, to witness the sunrise, "which is many-hued, like the rainbow, *they say*", adds the *Life*, for it was not the custom of Romans to take note of the beauties of nature, even though most of them did rise at dawn.

Back in Rome, after an absence of over five years, Hadrian found much to occupy him. First, there were his reforms, in the law and in administration. All was going well: the new model was working. So the emperor could turn to projects which were near his artist's heart. Not that he omitted the daily round. He was as assiduous as ever in attending the sessions of the senate' and in sitting as a magistrate. He liked attending parties, too, and meeting his friends informally. Everything came up for discussion, mathematics, the arts, painting, music: Hadrian fancied himself both as a singer and as a flautist. As a boy he must have heard much music, for Andalusia, and especially Cadiz, was then, as now, famous for its songs, its dances, and the plangent rhythm of the castanets. He knew all the tricks of the gladiator's trade, even. And, as we have seen, he liked writing poetry. Generally he addressed his verses to his love of the moment, but sometimes he could turn out a squib. For instance, when a friend of his called Florus sent him the following:

> "I don't want to be a Caesar
> Sauntering among the Britons,
> Lying low among the Germans,
> Putting up with Scythian winters,"

Hadrian at once came back with:

> "I don't want to be a Florus
> Sauntering among the taverns,
> Lying low among the cook-shops,
> Putting up with fat mosquitoes."

Hadrian the architect was anxious to see how his buildings, the ones he had designed before he set out, had come on during his absence. It seems impossible that a man who was already an accomplished general, an administrator of genius, a statesman of novel foresight, could add yet another claim to eminence. One could expect Hadrian's architecture to be dilettante, amateurish. That is certainly how it appeared to some of his professional contemporaries. Unfortunately, he had, as a boy, been rebuked by one of them, Apollodorus of Damascus, the man who had designed Trajan's greatest works, including the Forum of which impressive relics still survive. Once when Trajan had been discussing a design with him, young Hadrian had butted in with some advice, whereupon the architect (harassed as architects always are in such circumstances) said to him, "Go away! Go back to painting cucumbers! You don't know what we're talking about." When Hadrian came to design his own buildings, he wanted to shew Apollodorus that he did know what he was talking about. So he sent him his plan for the temple of Venus and Rome, which was to be the city's largest temple, and asked him what he thought of it. This temple, as Plate 10 makes clear, stood at the beginning of the Sacred Way, and opposite to the Colosseum. It was begun in the year 121, and in order to clear the site Hadrian had to remove a colossal statue of Nero, ninety-nine feet high, to a position nearer the Colosseum, where traces of its foundation may still be seen. Twenty-four elephants were needed to shift this graven image, keeping it upright all the time. Hadrian replaced Nero's head with one of the sun-god, to whom he rededicated it, and bade Apollodorus construct a twin statue to the moon. The temple took many years to build and was not consecrated until 135. When Hadrian sent him the plans, Apollodorus replied that it ought to be raised on a podium, both in order to be better seen from the Sacred Way, and also so that the vaults could be used for assembling and storing the machinery used in the adjacent theatre. He said, too, that the statues were too big for the shrine. "If the goddesses wanted to get up and go out, they'd hit their heads on the ceiling." The chronicler goes on to say that Hadrian was so annoyed that he first of all banished Apollodorus and then had him executed. This is hardly credible; it sounds like malicious gossip: as the plate shews, Hadrian did adopt the suggestion about the podium, and Apollodorus was active and busy some years later (see page 164). But the main design of this remarkable temple is his. The innovation of a double apse to the *cella*, in honour of the twin deities of the dedication, was a daring departure from conventional design. The twin ten-columned porticoes which it necessitated must have created a grand impression, standing there immediately opposite the great rotundity of the Colosseum, the static opposite the rhythmic (see Figure 1).

This contrast of the vertical static with the cylindrical rhythmic is the basic principle of Hadrian's masterpiece, the Pantheon. The first Pantheon had been built by Marcus Vipsanius Agrippa, Augustus' son-in-law and minister but it had been gutted by fire in the year 80 (see page 20). The present building bears Agrippa's name; and that has caused much misunderstanding almost up to our own day. It was only in 1892 that the French architect, Georges Chadanne, by making soundings in the masonry, established that the whole of it is built of bricks stamped (as was the Roman custom) with indications of dates between the years 120 and 125, and in particular 123 "in the consulship of Paetinus and

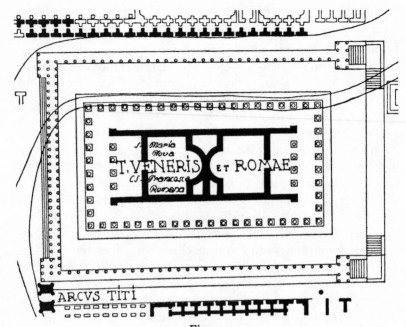

S. Maria
Nova
T. VENERIS ET ROMAE
CS. Francae
Romana

ARCVS TITI

Figure 1

(cf. Plate 10)

COS

Figure 2

Aproprianus". (See Fig. 2.) As was his custom Hadrian had put the founder's name, not his own, on the new buildings, even though it was his own work. During the past half century there has been a good deal of discussion about other parts of the building, especially the porch, which some thought a survival of Agrippa's building, and others regarded as part of a restoration by Septimius Severus, more than two centuries later, which shews how widely scholars can differ. But now it is generally admitted that the whole building is the work of one man and that its architect was Hadrian himself. The case is stated by Dr. Roberto Vighi, the foremost living authority on Hadrianic architecture, as follows (*The Pantheon*, tr. by J. G. Ward Perkins, Rome, 1957):

"The very character of the Pantheon suggests that Hadrian himself was its architect. Only one such as he was, at one and the same time an impassioned admirer of Greek culture and art and a daring innovator in the field of Roman architecture, could have conceived this union of a great pedimental porch in the Greek manner and of a vast circular hall, a masterpiece of architecture typically Roman in its treatment of curvilinear space, and roofed with the largest dome ever seen." (It is still the largest dome in the world, its diameter being 43.30 metres against St. Peter's 42.52.) "Considerations such as these justify our holding that the attribution of the plan of the Pantheon to Hadrian is still the most reasonable and likely hypothesis. It would moreover explain one or two not altogether stylish details, which suggest a certain lack of harmony between the intention of the design and the effect actually achieved, and which are just what one might expect from one who was not himself a professional architect." For example, the porch, which is not integrated with the rotunda, and the upper pediment, which is gauche.

Before examining the building in more detail, it may be helpful to state in general terms the aim of Hadrian's architectural innovation. As has been noted, Hadrian wanted his buildings to be impressive, imperial and grand. One of the essentials of such buildings is height. Now height is the one thing which Greek buildings do not possess. The Greeks thought and designed horizontally. The measure of all things, with them, was man: and so they designed their temples on a human scale, and constructed buildings in which man would be at home. They sited their temples perfectly, and placed them where they would be conspicuous. But they were not interested in aspiration, in soaring to heaven. They would not have understood the idea. Their buildings were to be perfect in themselves, without reference to any other world or state. When the Romans adapted Greek architecture to their own more grandiose requirements, all they could think of, at first, was to make the columns taller and the cornices heavier. And it was this spirit that eventually produced such monuments as the temple of the Sun at Baalbek or the temple of Zeus Olympios at Athens. But it could not be done indefinitely—the results, all too often, looked stringy, "leggy". Hadrianic architecture solved this problem, and surmounted the inherent defect, by turning away from the Greek columned orders to the solid, engineer-built brick buildings of Rome, for as engineers the Romans were paramount. This had already been done, in a tentative way, in the great theatres of Marcellus and the Colosseum, where the Greek orders are simply *appliqués* on a Roman mass: the columns themselves have as much relation to the building as those which used to adorn the steel-frame hotels of the nineteen-thirties. Hadrian saw that this "vestigial" use of the orders was the signpost to a dead end. Just as twentieth-century architects were one day to do, Hadrian took his eyes off the past and fixed them on his materials and the scientific skill available to use them to the best advantage. Taking the good brickwork and the scientific vaulting of Roman "functional" work, he evolved his own beautiful rhythmic version of it, and varied and elevated a science into an art. One analogue in our own century is the evolution of the skyscraper from a classical pier-and-cornice structure (of which the last, *reductio ad absurdum* example is the old Flat Iron building in New York) to an aspiring unity, governed by its own laws of proportion.

Once again, Hadrian was anticipating future achievements. It was the discovery of the pendentive (or how to place a round dome on a square base) in the Levant in the second century that sent architecture soaring, and made practical the Byzantine dome, of which St. Sophia is the supreme example; but it was Hadrian's genius that made the first flight, as it were. To realise how original he was it is only necessary to contemplate the surviving work of his immediate successors, for example the temple of Antoninus and Faustina, with its asparagus pillars, and bogus Greek aspect.

Rome. The Pantheon. Detail, shewing (a) the intricate
brickwork, with built-in relieving arches and (b) the clumsy
articulation of portico and rotunda—the mark of its amateur
architect (page 111).

Rome. The Pantheon. Interior, looking south towards what is now the high altar (page 113).

"The Pantheon," to quote Vighi again, "is composed of two quite distinct parts, a columned porch and a huge circular, domed *cella*, of which the *cella* is unquestionably the dominant element, suggesting that the cult-requirements were correspondingly greater than in any temple dedicated to a single divinity. Here the essential part of the temple is the *cella*, and the porch appears almost as an afterthought, added to give the building a façade and, by its use of traditional forms, to declare its purpose." Here again, Hadrian was an innovator. In traditional temples, the *cella*, the room designed to house the cult-god (of which the empty Holy of Holies of the Jerusalem Temple was the equivalent), was, from the aesthetic point of view, the least important part of the building, because the public never entered it. What they saw was the outside of the temple, and so it was on the exteriors of ancient temples, on their porticoes and courtyards, that the architects lavished their invention and skill. It is to this fact that we owe the *colonnade*, which became the feature of the temple *par excellence*. From that tradition, Hadrian, in his Pantheon, his temple of all the gods, broke away, thus anticipating the church of the Christians by several centuries.

A detailed description of the Pantheon would need a book in itself. Only a few comments can be offered here.

The porch, whatever its purpose, and although it may be an afterthought, is remarkably impressive, almost oppressive, as though its intention were to bring those who enter the temple to a state of humility. It stood originally at the top of a flight of five steps. It consists of a pedimented roof, supported by no less than sixteen monolithic columns, eight of grey Egyptian granite across the front, three on either flank, and two behind them on each side (see Plate 12). Each shaft is 12.50 metres high and 1.48 in diameter, with bases and capitals of white marble. Each shaft weighs about sixty tons. Seven of the columns in the front row come, as Professor Scaife has shewn, from Jebel Fitiry in the eastern desert of Egypt, where the imperial porphyry also came from. These quarries were opened up by Trajan, which rules out any possibility of the porch's being part of the original structure. They have Corinthian capitals which are among the finest in the whole range of Roman architecture.

The rotunda itself, which looks such a straightforward structure, is in fact a web of relieving arches, and variegated strata, which make it as complicated as a girder. It is scientifically balanced so as to take the strains of the dome. The dome itself is in reality an enormous concrete cup. The brilliance of its construction lies in the fact that it gradually diminishes in thickness towards the top, and that whereas the lower portions of it are made of a concrete containing brick and stone, in the uppermost, the concrete is made of pumice, that is of the lightest substance available.

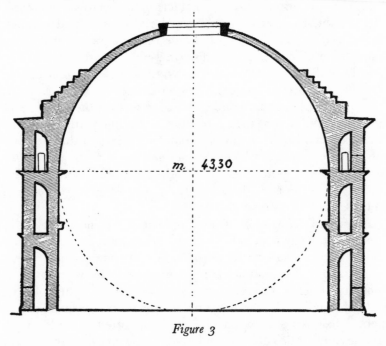

Figure 3

It is the interior that is the most magical part of the whole fabric. As Figure 3 shows, it is designed on a perfect circle, its diameter being exactly the same as its height. It is this perfect round that gives the building its sense of heavenly tranquillity and grandeur, that and the lighting, which comes solely from the opening at the summit of the dome, nearly nine metres wide. There is neither shadow nor shade, but everything is illuminated equally and evenly. The surface of the cylindrical wall was divided originally into three members, as may be seen in Plate 14. The lowest was enlivened by eight large recesses, the two at the entrance and the apse opposite it being arched, the remaining six screened by columns of exquisite marbles, brought from North

Africa and Asia Minor. Between the recesses stand *aedicules*, or "little temples". The *aedicule* had been in use for some time as a decorative detail, for example in the bas-relief of Augustus' Altar of Peace; but it was Hadrian who promoted it to the status of an individual architectural unit. The object of the *aedicules* in the Pantheon is to give variety, and also, by their subtly diminished scale, to stress the immensity of the superincumbent mass. The *aedicule* became a favourite feature with later classical architects, and may be seen in London in the upper storey of Wren's St. Paul's or in the windows of Barry's Travellers' and Reform Clubs in Pall Mall. This lowest of the three members of the wall was surmounted by a richly carved frieze, which runs sheer round the interior, binding the whole together. Above, there was an attic with delicate pilasters set off by false windows. This attic, which shews clearly enough in the sketches of Raphael (who is buried here) and of Piranesi, in the eighteenth century, was later obscured with the lifeless makeshift that we now see, except in one small section, where the original has been restored. Above rises the great coffered dome.

Shelley, writing to his friend Peacock in 1819, says of the Pantheon: "It is, as it were, the visible image of the universe; in the perfection of its proportions, as when you regard the unmeasured dome of heaven, the idea of magnitude is swallowed up and lost. It is open to the sky, and its wide dome is lighted by the ever-changing illumination of the air. The clouds of noon fly over it, and at night the keen stars are seen through the azure darkness, hanging immovably, or driving after the driven moon among the clouds."

Hadrian's Rome must have been a stimulating city to live in. On all hands new buildings arose, old ones were restored. Yet on only one of them, the temple of deified Trajan, did Hadrian place his own name, and that, in the case of his adoptive father, was a matter of piety, not of ostentation. The old voting lobby, the Basilica of Neptune, the Forum of Augustus, the baths of Agrippa behind the Pantheon, the temple of Bona Dea, the augurs' pavilion on the Palatine, all these Hadrian restored, in the names and to the honour of their founders. Of them all, only a few puzzling stones now remain.

But the Pantheon does not stand quite alone as a memorial of Hadrian's genius. His other great surviving building in Rome calls forth less enthusiasm, although it is probably known to far more people than the Pantheon. It is Hadrian's Mausoleum, which, as the Castel Sant' Angelo, has had such a vivid and sombre history, and as the setting of the last act of Puccini's *Tosca* is familiar to thousands who have never seen Rome nor heard of Hadrian. The building was not begun until three years before Hadrian's death, that is in 135, and was completed by his successor Antoninus, but it will be convenient to consider it here. Even in death, Hadrian was determined to imitate Augustus, and so his tomb must resemble Augustus' tomb. But just as Hadrian's buildings were more splendid than those of Augustus, so should his sepulchre outshine that of his model. Augustus had been buried in a stone rotunda, down by the Tiber, on the Campus Martius, and so had all his successors up to Nerva, in 98. It was now full. This monument, or what remains of it, was cleared and restored by Benito Mussolini in 1942. It was, ironically enough, his last civic achievement. The site is not a worthy one, and is also liable to flooding. Hadrian decided to go one better. His tomb also should be a rotunda, but he would erect it on a more conspicuous site, and ensure that it would not be flooded—there had been disastrous floods of recent years. He therefore decided to place it on the right bank of the Tiber, just where the river bends sharply, and to connect it to the city by a bridge. This is the Pons Aelius, of which the three central arches still survive in the modern bridge. It made, as it still makes, the perfect approach to the great monument, of which the Tiber thus becomes the forecourt, as it were. Beyond, there was laid out a square foundation, eighty-four metres long on each side, which the present walls of the fortress largely represent, and on it was placed the rotunda, slightly smaller in diameter than that of Augustus, which must have looked rather squat, but a good deal higher than it, about sixty feet from base to summit. The great drum was faced with marble, and crowned with statues. In the middle was a roof-garden, on the old Babylonian model. What crowned the edifice we have no idea, perhaps a quadriga or a colossal statue, or even the great bronze pine-cone which now forms the centre-piece of one of the courts of the Vatican Museum.

The interior was as austere and simple as death itself. An inscription to Hadrian and Sabina originally surmounted the portal. Immediately inside the door (which was ten feet lower than the present one) there was a vestibule, in which a niche housed a statue of the emperor, and from it, on the right, led a ramp, which in an anti-clockwise spiral makes a complete circuit of the building in the course of a hundred and twenty-five metres and rises twelve metres. This passage, which is beautifully constructed of travertine, was originally lined with marble. Its floor was covered with a simple black-and-white mosaic, and the ceiling was frescoed. This passage leading to the cell was no doubt inspired by the long adits which lead to the tombs of the Egyptian Pharaohs, and is a clever adaptation of that device for instilling awe.

At the end of the ramp a short transverse gallery leads to the *cella*, in the very heart of the whole mass. It was here that the urns containing the ashes of Hadrian, of Sabina and of his successors were placed. The urns and much else were looted by Alaric's horde in 410. In 537 the last of the statues were used as missiles to hurl down upon the besieging Goths. With the later history of the Mausoleum we are not concerned. It has largely transformed its structure. Only in this cold corridor and in this forlorn and ravished cell, only here in the very core of the building, is the visitor possessed by the grandeur of Rome and the mastery of death.

Chapter XV

AFRICA

AFTER little more than a year in Rome, the busy emperor was off again on his travels. This time it was *Africa*—the small Roman province corresponding to the modern Tunisia, which claimed him first. There were several reasons for this priority, as it would now be called. First, it was a frontier province, but, like Mauretania, a region where it was not easy to define a frontier. As we have seen in the case of the wall, what Hadrian liked was a definite, material line—a *limes*, a physical limit. The *Life* tells us that in Germany, where rivers did not constitute a natural barrier, Hadrian erected a palisade of stakes, and vestiges of such a one have been found between the Main and the Neckar, where the rivers themselves formed the frontier. But Hadrian was clever enough to see that in Africa no such limit could be defined. The sown must be protected from the desert by other means. In 1940, a great general (who in his many-splendoured genius bore a strong resemblance to Hadrian), when he was called to command the armies of the desert, put into effect a principle that he had laid down in a lecture a year earlier—that in mobile warfare the soldier must learn from the sailor, and conduct his operations as though they were sea battles. Hadrian had adopted this principle in part in his wall strategy, where the wall itself had the function of the modern aircraft-carrier—the base from which his forces could strike, instantly and in concentration. Africa must be treated in the same way, for Africa, small though it was geographically, was vital, because the possessor of Africa could, if hostile and strong, chop the Mediterranean in two. Had not Carthage done it? Carthage! The great, the hereditary enemy. That city, too, he must visit, the first Roman imperator to do so since Scipio.

Antiquarian lure was one reason for visiting this ancient land. There were two others. Africa was very fertile, and was one of the provinces that fed Rome. Its corn, its olive oil, were famous and abundant. The olive was of great importance in antiquity, because it was used not only for cooking, but also for lighting and washing. It was the ancient equivalent of both electricity and soap. Africa also produced wild beasts.

The sea journey was shorter from Carthage than from other ports on the coast, and so it was from there that the thousands of creatures were exported to be terrified and butchered in the Roman arenas. Every age has a "blind defect"—some taint that is quite incongruous with its prevailing moral standards. In eighteenth-century England, it was slavery, in the twentieth, belief in bombs. Hadrian's age had a great many, but Hadrian himself had not. So it is all the more repellent to find that this sensitive man, who could have the whole theatre strewn with balsam and saffron, to make it smell nice, should nevertheless revel in the slaughter of hundreds of tortured beasts. They were supplied by contractors, who did very well out of this horrible trade. At Piazza Armerina, in Sicily, there is the villa of one such man, and the floors of his palace, for it is no less, are paved with mosaics, some of which depict the catching and shipping of his merchandise. In their profusion and variety, they look like an old-fashioned picture of Noah's ark.

Finally, the legion that was stationed in Africa was the IIIrd, Augusta, "Caesar's Own", as we should say. Caesar must inspect it.

It would be hard to overestimate the impact of Carthage upon Hadrian. Here he was, in the very capital of the one and only empire which had rivalled that of Rome, of the people who had overrun Greek Sicily, who had even lorded it over Hadrian's native land of Spain. For more than a century Rome had fought Carthage, in three long wars, during the second of which, "the war of a man with a nation" in Arnold's phrase, Hannibal had brought Rome to the very brink of ruin. "Carthage must be destroyed," went up the cry; and, in 146 B.C., it was. But the memory remained. Virgil, in one of his noblest passages, one of the few in ancient literature that deal with human emotion in a modern, "psychological" way, makes Aeneas, the hero-founder of Rome, desert Dido. To present-day readers the man seems a cad. Not so to the Romans: Dido was a Carthaginian; of course a decent Roman would awake from so lascivious a dream, and quit her. Cleopatra was detested in Rome, not because she had captivated first Caesar and then Antony, but because she was, in Roman eyes, another Dido.

The Carthaginians were Semites. The name of their town in

their own language might have come from the Bible: it was *Kirjath-Hadeshat*, the New Town, to distinguish it from Tyre, whence its founders had come, or the earlier settlement of Utica. When Hadrian landed, he found himself, for the first time, in a province of his empire whose inhabitants spoke as their vernacular, not one of the two imperial languages, Latin or Greek, but their own, Phoenician tongue. As a boy, in Italica, he had heard about these people, he had probably seen some of them. But to find that they still existed in large numbers, and still preserved their national language, must have been a shock, and an affront, to the Greek-Roman emperor. What would be his attitude to their cousins, the Jews, when in due course he came in contact with them? Hadrian's antipathy to the Jews undoubtedly had its roots in his revulsion from the Carthaginians.

Hadrian, who almost never put his own name on his monuments, must have taken a particular pleasure in renaming Hannibal's city Hadrianopolis. He visited Zama, the site of the Roman Waterloo, Scipio's victory over Carthage, and Utica the scene of the death of the last Roman republican, Cato, of whom the Roman poet had sung, "Heaven chose the winning cause, Cato the lost." Hadrian affected to admire his style more than that of Cicero. Both these towns were made into Roman colonies. And to shew that Heaven was now on the side of Hadrian, it rained for the first time for five years. Truly he was the harbinger of blessing and plenty.

Hadrian then moved south, to the newly established frontier fort on the fringe of the desert, the unknown, at Lambaesis. Hadrian himself might have uttered Lyautey's *mot*: "*J'aime les soldats, je déteste les militaires.*" ("I love soldiers, I hate the military" does not quite catch the contrast.) He wanted to be with his troops, as a soldier, and the leading soldier of his age. So he went and lived in camp for a fortnight. He could see for himself how the army was behaving, how his new regulations were being observed, and how that new and lighter equipment which Apollodorus had designed for them was working out. By good fortune, the base of a monumental column erected at Lambaesis has in part survived, and on it, excerpts from five addresses which Hadrian made to the troops. No doubt the regiments only preserved the best and most flattering bits, but they are of considerable interest—the first of countless allocutions by inspecting generals. For instance, to the men of "Caesar's Own" he says that their colonel had explained to him that the regiment was not up to strength owing to so many men being absent on detachment, some seconded to other units, and many on picket duty at the various frontier posts. And they had only recently moved in, and had had to construct the camp themselves. "All these factors would be excuse enough, if your drill or manoeuvres had fallen short in any respect. On the contrary, you need no excuse. Your colonel has been tireless in his care for you. Your N.C.O.s have proved themselves as smart and brave as ever . . ."

The cavalry get their bouquet, too. "All military exercises have precise and definite rules laid down for them. If anything is taken away or added, the exercise becomes either useless or too involved. The more elaborate an exercise is, the poorer show it makes. You chose to demonstrate to me the hardest of all, javelin throwing at full gallop and in full armour. I congratulate you on your keenness." The auxiliaries, too, were commended, the mounted infantry from Spain, the horse from what are now Austria and eastern Turkey. The address to the mounted infantry is of particular interest, because it shews the Roman soldier in his rôle of pioneer, and gives us a glimpse of the method by which Hadrian's wall must have been built. Here it is, in Henderson's translation:

"Entrenchment which others take many days to construct you finished in a single day. You built a wall quite good enough for permanent winter-quarters in a time hardly longer than that wanted for a rampart of sods of earth. This last kind of rampart is quite an easy matter. The turfs are cut of a standard size, and are easy to carry and to handle. There is no difficulty in placing them one on top of another, for they are naturally soft and level. But the wall which you built was of big heavy stones of all shapes and sizes, and to lift or carry these and to put them in place they have to be very carefully fitted together. Next, you cut a trench in a plumb straight line through the very hardest and coarsest gravel, and made its sides perfectly smooth as well. When you had done this, back you went full tilt to camp, got your rations and your arms, and out you sallied at once after the cavalry. When you found these falling back on you, you advanced with loud cheers in their support . . . I compliment my legate Catullinus on his choice of manoeuvres so like real warfare for your training, and for prac- tising you so well in these that I am able to congratulate you all very heartily on the result. Cornelianus, too, your own commander, is an excellent officer . . .

"I do not myself care much for open order tactics, and in this I follow the best authority. In advance, the trooper should make all the use he can of cover; and in pursuit he should exercise caution. Otherwise, unless he looks where he is going and is able to rein in sharply whenever he wants, he may easily find himself trapped . . . When you charge, let it be knee to knee . . ."

The battered, defaced pillar of Lambaesis is more eloquent than any book. We can see and hear the general, proud of his Spaniards, proud, too, of his soldier's lore and experience. The good Catullinus had his reward. He was a consul two years later.

Africa was an important granary, and therefore it must be made to produce as abundantly as possible. So long as the nomads roamed over the country, with their sheep and goats, agriculture was impossible. The Romans, as they occupied and stabilized the country, did exactly what the Italian Fascists were later to do when they in their turn occupied Cyrenaica: they simply expelled the nomads from the best land and planted colonies therein. From the practical point of view, the scheme was a success; and today we can see in areas which are now desert the relics of Roman farms, the oil-presses and the silos, even (from the air) the very pattern of the olive-groves, long since desolate and barren. There is also evidence of Hadrian's vivifying presence in the two great Libyan towns of Leptis Magna and Sabratha. In the former the baths bear the mark of his invention. They are modelled on the largest imperial baths of Rome, but with individual touches. They cover more than seven acres. The major rooms are on the grand axis, the plunge-bath, the cool room, the hot room. On the sides are the changing-rooms, individual baths, etc. An annexe housed the latrines and the *palaestra*. This had an apse at each end, and was decorated with a wealth of marbles and mosaics, and with excellent reproductions of masterpieces of classical statuary, such as Hadrian always insisted on.

The people of Sabratha became so prosperous that they had their own establishment in the Square of the Corporations at Ostia: it was, as we may observe today, "at the sign of the Elephant". And in the Forum at Rome has been found a dedication to the empress Sabina, the gift of the grateful citizens of this remote African city.

Chapter XVI

ATHENS REVISITED—THE EASTERN QUESTION

IT was in the height of summer that Hadrian had visited Africa, and had watched the army manoeuvres, bare-headed beneath the torrid sun. He returned direct to Rome, but he did not stay there long. He was agog for Athens. In Rome he hated the court etiquette, at the same time as he insisted on it: the wearing of the toga, the formal greetings, the ceremonies, the endless pressure of business. Sometimes he became petulant. Once, as he was setting out for an official function, a woman came up to him with a petition. Hadrian brushed her aside—"I have no time," he said. "Then you've no right to rule," answered the woman, and Hadrian heard her out. On the other hand, he could be facetious. Once a grey-haired man came to him with some request, and Hadrian turned it down. A few days later the man came back, this time with dyed hair, and repeated his request. "I have already refused it to your father," said Hadrian—a remark which is recorded as an example of his wit.

In Athens Hadrian really did feel at ease. He donned Greek dress, and talked Greek. This time, he had the satisfaction of presenting himself as more Greek than ever. He took the final degree of initiation at Eleusis—he had taken the first degree on his previous visit. He presided at his new Panhellenic council, and the Panhellenic games, where he might behold the most handsome athletes of all Hellas competing in boxing and other contests. The Panhellenic council had no political status; but it gave the Greeks a sense of unity, of personality, because it was this body which issued the certificate which declared that a community, perhaps in Asia, was truly Hellenic. In view of twentieth-century manifestations of Greek nationalism in lands far distant from Greece, this precedent is not without interest. Hadrian himself liked to be called *Panhellenios*.

Hadrian's buildings were now nearing completion. The new city, Hadrianopolis, had arisen round the great temple of Zeus. It was entered by a monumental gateway (see Plate 9). This is un-doubtedly Hadrianic in design—the *aedicule* immediately above the arch proclaims it—but it must be accounted among his less successful productions: it lacks solidity, though when it was first built, the upper spaces, now open, were filled with marble partitions and statues; it is, like certain of Nash's buildings in London, or Suleiman's Damascus Gate in Jerusalem, more theatrical than architectural. This, probably, because it attempts too blatantly to harmonise the curvilinear Roman with the rectilinear Greek. The arch is just over twenty feet wide. On the frieze is written, on one side: "This is the city of Theseus, the former city", and on the other "This is of Hadrian, and not the city of Theseus". His new bridge spanned the Cephisus, his canals had tamed the Ilissus. His gymnasium was a masterpiece. One of the best surviving examples of a Greek gymnasium is at Salamis, in Cyprus. It is no mere hall, or building. It is a spacious *piazza*, more than two hundred feet square, with a colonnade all round it, and baths and exercise rooms on the four sides. It is, in fact, so large and splendid that until recent excavations proved its real function, it was believed to be a market-place. Hadrian's gym-nasium at Athens was of the same sort. It had no less than one hundred pillars in its colonnade, all of them brought from Libya. It was more than a hundred yards long in each direction; and it incorporated the Propylaea of Augustus. Then there was his Stoa, or Portico, which contained among other things his public library. This also was a quadrangle, four hundred feet by two hundred and seventy, also embellished with a hundred columns, from Phrygia. On all sides stood statues of the emperor; the theatre of Dionysus, where Hadrian had presided at the Dionysia on his previous visit, had twelve. There were four statues of him in front of the great Olympieum, two of stone from Thasos, two of Egyptian granite. There was a colossal statue of him at the back.

The temple itself must have been overwhelming. Of its more than one hundred columns fifteen are still standing. To anyone acquainted with Hadrian's architectural style, they present a puzzling question, because they seem to embody the very faults in Roman architecture, when it tried to be Greek, that were described earlier (see page 112). How then could it be Hadrian's work? The answer is that its plan is not Hadrian's work. When

Antiochus had started it, he had employed a Roman architect, Cossutius, who had produced just the sort of elongated, over-reaching columniation that the Romans liked; the full height of the façade was some ninety feet, or higher than the roof of King's College chapel. Hadrian had merely completed the original design. Inside there was a colossal statue of Zeus, of gold and ivory, "Worth seeing", says Pausanias, who adds that "considering its size, the workmanship is good". Only the Colossus of Rhodes, and the Colossus of Nero, which Hadrian had moved to make room for his temple of Venus and Rome (see page 109), were larger.

The whole effect must have been remarkably impressive, even though vulgar. The temple is far enough away from the Acropolis not to clash with the Parthenon, to which it bears about the same relationship as Waterloo station does to Inigo Jones' Whitehall Banqueting House.

Polemo was invited to deliver the address at the consecration service. He rose, advanced to the plinth of the temple, put on a thoughtful and faraway look, and delivered a long and fluent oration: such a theme, he said, was an inspiration in itself. Hadrian dedicated as his oblation a gift which appears from the description of it given by Dio to have been a representation of a snake, or mythical animal, from India, probably of gold encrusted with jewels.

Hadrian himself was now hailed as "Olympian", and the grateful Athenians named one of their tribes after him.

For Hadrian and for Athens alike, it had been an enchanted winter. Never, since the great days of Pericles, had Athens known such radiance, nor Hadrian, in all his life, such satisfaction. At Olympia, the paradise of athletes near Arcadia, where the ephebes of today still exercise naked on the banks of the Alpheus, and refresh themselves in its waters, there stands a statue of Hadrian which is of great significance. It is an official monument, and the emperor is therefore represented, according to custom, wearing the *lorica*, or breastplate, on which, also according to custom, would be graven some theme illustrative of the emperor's character. Hadrian's *lorica* shews Athene, flanked by her owl and her snake, being crowned by two graces, and standing atop the Wolf of Rome which suckles Romulus and Remus. Nothing could illustrate more clearly Hadrian's view of the relative status of

Athens and Rome, but it could hardly have pleased the eyes of any Roman who happened to visit Olympia.

In March 129 the emperor was on his way once more to Asia, accompanied this time by Sabina. On all hands he was hailed as "saviour" and "founder"—coins from at least thirty-seven cities of Asia Minor attest it. Sabina was addressed as the new Hera. The royal suite landed at Ephesus, visited the coast of Caria, where Halicarnassus, the birthplace of Herodotus, must have been an attraction, and journeyed along the Southern Highway to Laodicea, and so on by south-west Phrygia to Lycia and Cilicia. Tarsus, the birthplace of St. Paul, took the title *Hadriane*, and so did Adana. The captain of the ship in which Hadrian had crossed the Aegean was not forgotten. Hadrian offered to pay the fees for his admission as a city councillor of Ephesus. There were the usual largesses to temples and towns. In Tralles a generous official distributed 15,000 bushels of grain from Egypt, to commemorate the imperial visit. By the middle of June Hadrian was back in Antioch, the city from which, eleven years earlier, he had set out as emperor for Rome. The town, lying at the foot of a lofty scarp, and washed by the Orontes, was superbly sited, and the neighbouring park of Daphne, refreshed by cascades of limpid water, shaded by overarching trees, is one of the most beguiling retreats in all Syria. Hadrian had donated an improved irrigation system (he was always fascinated by water) with a temple and bath, and these were now formally inaugurated. And yet Hadrian was not happy in Antioch. For all its Greekness—it had been the Seleucid capital for nigh on three centuries, and it was the third city of the empire—there was something distasteful about it. The fact was, that despite all the foreign veneer, Antioch remained Semitic. The inhabitants spoke Aramaic, a language closely akin to Punic, and the *lingua franca* of the whole region from Persia to Egypt. It was the language of our Lord and of his disciples. It is spoken to this day in three villages near Damascus. These Semites, how tough, how unteachable they were! (How tough they were may be seen in their place-names; Akko, for instance, was known as Ptolemais, in honour of the Greek Ptolemies, for close on a millennium. But with the advent of the Arabs, it reverted to its original name, and to this day is called 'Akka. Only new foundations, such as Sebaste, retained their new names.)

Hadrian decided to take Antioch down a peg. He proposed to

separate the province of Phoenicia from Syria, and make it a separate command. This was actually only done in the reign of Septimius Severus, some eighty years later; but Hadrian did elevate the city of Tyre to the status of metropolis of Phoenicia, and similarly Damascus for the Lebanon, and Samosata, on the Euphrates for Commagene, the north-eastern sector of the province. Antioch, thus shorn of some of its importance, remained the provincial capital. In the autumn Hadrian visited Cappadocia, to inspect the legion stationed at Melitene (now Malathe), the XIIth, Thunderbolt, and to obtain some slaves to serve the army. Cappadocia had until A.D. 17 been an independent kingdom. It had been feudally organised, so that slaves were plentiful. Hadrian realised that if his new model army was to be really efficient it should be relieved of as many non-military tasks as possible. Hence this recruitment of Cappadocian slaves.

On his way back Hadrian stopped at Samosata (now Samsat), headquarters of the XVth, Flavians. He had decided to tackle the "Eastern Question", that is Rome's relations with Parthia. Nothing in Roman history is of more interest to a modern reader than the long, complicated, and often mysterious story of her rivalry with Parthia—mysterious, because, as in the case of Rome's dealings with Carthage, or those of the Jews with the Philistines, we have only one side of the story.

Rome had won an empire. That empire was a Roman estate. It was protected by a fence of frontiers. Within was civilisation, without barbarism. That was the Roman imperial conception. Rome had no equals, no rivals. To this formula there was one exception—Parthia. The Parthians were not barbarians, they were highly civilised, as their Persian forebears had been, long before Rome was. The Parthians were also, and this the Romans respected more, very powerful. Even in republican times, during the expansionist ardour of the first century B.C., Rome had clashed with Parthia. Pompey had met her army. In 53 B.C. Crassus had been utterly routed by it, with the loss of seven legions. It was the most humiliating defeat Rome had ever suffered. Mark Antony's attempt at conquest had been a farce and a failure. Julius Caesar planned an expedition, but died before it could be mounted. Augustus, the cold, prudent administrator, realised that diplomacy, not war, was the answer to the Parthian problem. He secured the return of the standards, and honour was deemed to be satisfied. Technically, the two nations were friends. Augustus was clever enough to see that whereas the empire, which meant, then as now, European influence and ideas, might extend as far as the Euphrates, Parthia was oriental, eastern, different. Rome had no desire to conquer Parthia. Parthia knew that she could not conquer the eastern portion of the empire. Here was a clear case for peaceful co-existence. For long periods it was maintained. Rome created a chain of buffer-states, or client kingdoms, as they were known, which stretched from the Black Sea right down to Judaea, except where Syria intervened. Syria was too rich to be left to indirect rule, and the desert was in itself an effective buffer. Gradually all but one of these states had been absorbed into Roman provinces, so that Rome and Parthia had a common frontier. The exception was Armenia, which marched with Parthia on the east and with Roman Cappadocia and Syria on the west and south. Armenia was culturally akin to Parthia, but was pulled this way and that by the rival powers. Who was to be the king of Armenia? A Roman nominee, a Parthian prince, or a "collaborator"? All three were tried. None succeeded. There had been a war with Parthia under Nero, in which Rome had again suffered defeat. Again, diplomacy repaired what the army had lost. Trajan had almost conquered Parthia, and had forced her to accept Roman suzerainty. But it was an uneasy situation. Hadrian felt that the time had come for generosity. He therefore sent back to king Chosroes the daughter whom Trajan had taken as a hostage thirteen years before. He also promised to return the golden throne which had been carried off on the same occasion. (This promise was not carried out either by Hadrian or by his successor Antoninus.) Peace was maintained and strengthened. So much so that when the next inevitable Armenian crisis arose in the following reign, Antoninus was able to prevent hostilities merely by a written appeal to the Parthian king.

At a time when the East-West relationship, in another permutation, is once again the preoccupation of Europe, this history of Rome's dealings with Parthia—and it goes on right up to the defeat of both by the Arabs—has a special and sombre attraction.

Hadrian scored another diplomatic success. He invited all the dynasts of the region between the Euphrates and the Caucasus to come and visit him. Most of them came, and he entertained them with such lavish magnificence that those who had stayed away regretted their churlishness. He even got the better of Pharasmanes, the king of the Iberi, who lived in what is now Georgia and had treated the invitation with haughty indifference. Hadrian sent him a number of rich presents, including an elephant and fifty soldiers. Pharasmanes replied with a consignment of gold-embroidered cloaks. Hadrian had three hundred condemned criminals dressed up in them, and sent them into the arena to kill each other, just to shew Pharasmanes what he thought of him and his presents. The lesson was not lost on Pharasmanes, who visited Rome with his queen during the next reign and shewed fitting respect both to Rome and to its ruler.

For Hadrian the nature-lover there were many pleasant excursions to make in the neighbourhood of Antioch. The man who, four years earlier, had climbed Mount Etna to see the sunrise, planned a similar ascent of Mount Casius, the peak over five thousand feet high which dominates the whole of northern Syria, and the sea, too, as far as Cyprus. He wanted to see the dawn, and then to offer a sacrifice to the mountain-god, Baal Saphon, now known as Zeus Casios. But he was to do neither: a storm of rain obscured the rising sun, and the sacrificial victim was struck by lightning. So was the acolyte. At once the official hierophants declared that this event proved that Hadrian was the best of monarchs, the elect of Jupiter. But to Hadrian himself, who was haunted by his belief in astrology, and like most Romans, lived in dread of the inauspicious, how chilling, in that bleak twilight, on that lonely mountain, must the omen have seemed. The sun was hidden, the offering consumed, the acolyte slain. What, in Hadrian's own life, could that portend? Could it be anything but woe?

Hadrian had eight more years to live; but they were to be tarnished by failure, sorrow and sickness. His sun, already, was in decline, and he was for the dark.

Chapter XVII

LEBANON AND ARABIA

IN the autumn of the year 129, Hadrian turned south, to set out
on what was to prove his most fatal voyage; the journey during
which he was to make inevitable a war with the Jewish people,
of which we yet in our own day feel the consequences, the journey
during which his favourite, Antinoüs, was to die in circumstances
which, even though wrongly, have ever since stained the reputation of his master.

But, as he left Antioch for Beirut, Hadrian had no premonition
of disaster. On the way he visited Palmyra, the rich oasis which
was now beginning to eclipse its southern rival, Petra, as the
entrepôt of the eastern trade, which the peace between Rome and
Parthia and the general rise in the standard of living within the
empire increasingly fostered. Rare woods and spices, rich textiles,
strange birds and beasts, exotic gems, and, luxury of luxuries, silk
itself, the coveted web that only China produced—all these now
began to flow through the customs posts and counting-houses of
the Palmyrenes, whose citizens, proud and opulent, still gaze at us
from their funerary monuments in the museum of Damascus. Their
features are cast in a Semitic mould, with here and there a touch
of the Greek. They had known which side to back, these canny
merchants, in the struggle between west and east, and their desert
corps, mounted on dromedaries, was enrolled among the allied
contingents of the Roman army. Hadrian was happy to be able to
inspect them, and to bestow the usual benefactions on the rising city.

From Palmyra, Hadrian made his way to the coast, by way of
Damascus. This ancient city was so delighted with the honour
which Hadrian had done it (see page 127) that it put the word
metropolis on its coins. It went further, it actually minted an issue
which hailed the emperor as Hadrian the god, and others with the
head of *Sabina Sebaste*, that is *Augusta*, whom the Greeks had
assimilated, as we have seen, with Demeter. This issue is of more
than passing interest. It could not have appeared without official
sanction. It must have found its way into Jewish hands, for there

was a large Jewish community in Damascus, and, such were the links, in that century as in our own, between Damascus and Palestine, it must have been seen with horror and apprehension in the Holy Land itself where, as we know from the Gospel, even the tribute money was an offence.

Beirut was a Roman colony, that is, a settlement, of Italian expatriates for the most part, who enjoyed Roman privileges, although they lived in a province. Beirut, or *Berytus* as the Romans called it, lying at the foot of the snow-topped Lebanon, between the blue sky and the blue sea, is the most Italian locality in all Phoenicia, and might almost persuade the Italian that he was home again. The citizens were pleased by Hadrian's visit, and to shew their gratitude they dedicated an offering to him in the temple of Baal Marqod at Deir al-Qala'. Hadrian had paid much attention to the question of improving the roads of Syria, as we learn from surviving milestones bearing his name. In the first year of his reign he had repaired the road from Baalbek to the south. Now he took in hand, as his French and British successors were in their turns to do, the reconstruction of the great southern trunk road, the oldest road in the world, the Way of the Sea, which led south to Sidon.

We possess an interesting and characteristic testimony of Hadrian's stay in the Lebanon. From time immemorial the forests of Lebanon had been a coveted asset. Neither in Mesopotamia, nor in Egypt—the centres of the world's first rival dynasties—is there any indigenous timber. The forests of Lebanon were therefore a prime objective for any ruler who aspired to maintain a navy. As early as the days of Artaxerxes I, five hundred years earlier, cutting the trees of the royal reserve was a sign of revolt, like a raid on an arsenal, so valuable were they. The trade in cedar wood had also its pacific purposes, as we know from the Bible story of Solomon and Hiram. Byblos and Tyre were the ports whence the Phoenicians carried the precious trees to Egypt and Judaea. By Hadrian's time, although the forests of Cyprus were now also at the disposal of Rome, the demand for good ship-timber and for elegant roof-beams was such that unless some measure of conservation were imposed, the mountain would soon become deforested. So it was ordained. Scores of notices, engraved on stone, were erected on the boundaries of the forests bearing, in full, or, like English bench-marks, abbreviated, the inscription: "Of the emperor Hadrian Augustus, four kinds of trees, the others handed over to private individuals—forest boundary." The notice is sometimes accompanied by a figure, which probably indicated the number of trunks reserved in each stand. There is a good example in the Museum of the American University in Beirut. The four reserved varieties would be the cedar, the pine, the cypress and the juniper.

Hadrian saved the cedars of Lebanon. In our own day, their shrunken progeny is being preserved and propagated by the Lebanese government.

From Phoenicia Hadrian turned east, to visit Arabia, Rome's newest province. As with Asia and Africa the term Arabia, was applied, in official Roman terminology, to a small part only of the region which we denote Arabia today, namely to what had been the kingdom of the Nabataeans, that is to say what in the twentieth century became known as Trans-Jordan and the Hauran. The Nabataeans were Arabs, and their capital was the famous city of Petra. They were traders, like the Palmyrenes, and they had become rich in the same way, by acting as middlemen in the eastern trade. For some time they had held a monopoly of it, until the Roman penetration of the Red Sea and the discovery by an Alexandrian sea-captain of the monsoon, both of which occurred in the days of Augustus, compelled them to share it with the west. Nevertheless, so great was the demand for spices and the products of the east in a prosperous and peaceful empire that the Nabataeans still remained extremely rich. For some time Rome had had her eye on the Nabataean kingdom, which had become one of her "client" states. And here it will be as well to point out a fundamental difference between Roman and English ideas of empire. No country has ever had a finer or more generous record in its dealings with other races than the English. No great power, since history began, has occupied, and advanced to autonomous sovereignty, so large an extent of territory in so short a period. The advance, it is true, was from the very first, when the American colonists set the precedent, encouraged by the inhabitants of the territory concerned; nevertheless, it did not take long for England to adopt as a principle that the aim of all colonial enterprise is the elevation of the colonials, and their establishment as independent states, in whatever form of association they may choose with Great Britain. Such is the British

Empire, or, in Lord Rosebery's famous phrase, the Common-wealth of Nations. To a Roman, this would have been rubbish. The object of Rome—had not her most famous poet said so?—was to rule, and to go on ruling. On the periphery of her domin-ions, puppet monarchs might be tolerated, and used—for a time. As Tacitus said, Rome made even kings the instruments of servi-tude; but in the end Rome would extinguish and annex. So it was in the Levant, where, one by one, all the client kingdoms had disappeared: Cappadocia, Commagene, Judaea, together with a number of "splinter" fiefs, they were all now Roman provinces. Armenia remained un-Roman for the reasons given in the last chapter. But for the Nabataean kingdom, once Trajan had started on his career of expansion in the east, there was no longer any hope of survival. In fact it had had three narrow escapes already. The first was in 63 B.C., when Pompey brought Roman arms to the east. He was about to invade the Nabataeans, when he was deflected to Jerusalem. His lieutenant accepted an "indemnity" to abandon the assault. Nearly seventy years later, Augustus had intended to present the kingdom to Herod the Great, but Herod died before the intention could have effect. Forty years later still, when the Nabataean king had made war on Herod Antipas, Rome's protégé, Tiberius ordered the governor of Syria to humble him. Once again, by the death of Tiberius, Petra was saved.

But in the year A.D. 106 this Arab kingdom at last became a Roman province, which also took in, on the west, some towns of the Decapolis, the famous Ten Cities of Greek settlers. At one time, as we know for instance, from II Cor. xi, 32, the rule of the Nabataeans had extended as far as Damascus, and so a con-siderable area in the north of the kingdom was now assigned to the province of Syria, which was, and still is, the natural market for the greater part of its abundant grain harvests. Roman rule was probably welcome to a number of the inhabitants, particu-larly in the northern part of the kingdom, where the agents of Rabbel II, the last king of Petra, must have seemed almost alien; it certainly was effected with very little trouble. The governor of Syria, Cornelius Palma, and the VIth, Ironclads, carried it out with so little opposition that the coins struck to celebrate the event tell of *Arabia adquisita*, Arabia *acquired*, not *captured*, and shew on the reverse an Arab standing with an olive branch in his hand and a camel at his feet. The capital of the new province was transferred from Petra to Bostra, near the northern border, in order that communications should be made easier, and the legion have more pleasant quarters than the romantic, but remote and rugged, Petra could afford. Next, a great arterial road was constructed, which ran from Damascus, to Bostra, Philadelphia ('Amman), and right down to 'Aqaba, on the Red Sea. This wonderful highway, of which sections still exist, justified the boast of its milestones, that it ran "open and paved, from the frontiers of Syria to the Red Sea". Its eastern flank, and that of the province, was protected from the Beduin, who now for the first time were beginning to be called *Saracens* (that is *sharqiin*, easterners, to distinguish them from Rome's "tame" Arabs), by a string of forts. Of these, too, considerable relics exist, and over some of them flies the flag of the Hashemite kingdom, whose desert patrols have replaced those of Rome. The great road, too, is being reconstructed. To wander in this lone land, and to contemplate these seemingly imperishable relics of Roman dominion, still enduring for the convenience of government and the protection of the peaceful, is to be possessed with an overpowering sense of the might of Rome. The visitor to Hadrian's wall experiences the same feeling. Two thousand miles separate the two barriers; but the same mind controlled them. Such must have been the proud thought in Hadrian's mind, when he made his way down to Petra. He called the city Hadriana, and conferred on it the honorofic *metropolis*. Among the famous rock-cut chambers, Hadrian saw, as we see today, the ancient tiered mausoleum known as the treasury, the sepulchre of a heroised king, and also one of the most recent tombs, that of the second imperial governor, Sextus Florentinus, who had died twenty-two years before, and of whose honours and achievements we may still read in the Latin inscription engraved on the façade.

From Petra and the desert frontier, Hadrian turned west, to the most beautiful of all the cities of the new province, Gerasa, or Jerash. Here he spent the greater part of the winter of 129-30. The city was one of the Decapolis, and surely never any Greek city had more Arcadian a setting. It lies athwart a stream, the Golden River, as it was called, in a fold of the rich and rolling upland that unites the citadel of Philadelphia with the oakwoods of 'Ajlun. It is a landscape, half wild, half tame, such as the Greek

painters and poets loved to depict. The city itself is better preserved than any other of its kind; and today we can walk along
the very same streets, beneath the very same arcades as Hadrian
did. We can also behold the great triumphal arch which a rich
citizen of Jerash, Flavius Agrippa, erected in honour of the
emperor at the southern approach to the city (see Plate 16). It is
impressive, even in ruin, and an interesting mixture of East and
West; the columns springing from acanthus leaf bases give a lush
effect which is very un-Roman. It was crowned, as its dedicatory
inscription records, with a quadriga, and must have proclaimed
a dazzling welcome to wayfarers from Philadelphia. Jerash, like
other towns of the region, had suffered during the Jewish war of
66-70, but it was now prosperous and expanding as a result of
the creation of the new province and the great trunk highway.
Hadrian seems to have proposed that here, as at Athens, a new
quarter, called after him, should come into being between the arch
and the existing town, and for this he provided the new wall and
the gate. It does not appear, however, that the plan was ever
carried into effect.

It was in 130, too, that another Hadrianic gateway was
completed, that of Attaleia or Adalia, the great port on the
southern shore of Asia Minor. From what remains of it, we can
judge that it was typical of its architect, its three great arches, like
those of a viaduct, being lightened in aspect by the four free-
standing pillars placed before them on either side. It was a
typically Hadrianic contrast of strength and grace, whose richness
suggests a fantasy of Veronese or Tiepolo.

Early in the next year, Hadrian, like Joshua of old, crossed the
Jordan, and entered Palestine. We are told that it was his habit
to map out, on the first day of January, the whole of the succeeding
year by astrological lore: he can hardly have foreseen the disasters
that were to come upon him in the year 130.

Chapter XVIII

JEWS AND CHRISTIANS

THE measures which Hadrian was now about to take in Palestine, his policy in regard to the Jews, their religion, and their Holy City, were to prove the most disastrous of his career, both for Rome and for the Jews as well. They were to have an influence on the future of Jewry, and of its relations with Christianity, which has lasted to our own day. It will be well, therefore, to examine very briefly the position of the Jews, and of the Christians, as they found themselves in the year A.D. 130.

"All our religion, almost all our law, almost all our art, almost all that sets us above savages, has come to us from the shores of the Mediterranean." Samuel Johnson's dictum perfectly defines the origin and nature of European culture: it is, in essence, a "Tale of Three Cities"—Athens, Jerusalem and Rome. They form the tripod, as it were, on which our civilisation rests, and it is well-nigh impossible for a modern European to imagine a society where Hellenism and Judaism were violently antagonistic to each other, where Rome, the very name that is now a synonym for the faith of Christ, was its enemy and oppressor. Yet such was the state of affairs when Hadrian became emperor.

From their first contact, Judaism and Hellenism had clashed. The Greeks thought horizontally, the Jews perpendicularly. Greek thought, like the architecture which expressed it (see Chapter XIV), concentrated on man as the measure of all things, as the ideal, not only in mind, but in body as well. Both mind and body must be revered as expressions of beauty, and this world, this only world, must be so ordered that man might lead the good life in it. The Jewish idea of the world, and of man's place in it, was quite different. To begin with, man was not the measure of all things: he was the humble servant of a supreme and sublime God. Of himself he was nothing: he could only become a personality in so far as he obeyed the commands of God. For ever his heart must be set on eternity, on the mandates of the Lord of Hosts. Fortunately for mankind, said the Jews, God had chosen one

Rome. Hadrian's mausoleum (Castel Sant' Angelo) from the Pons Aelius, with the dome of St Peter's in the background (page 116).

Jerash. Triumphal gateway erected for Hadrian (page 135).

Cyrene. This magnificent inscription, in the Baths, reads as follows: "The emperor Trajan Hadrian Caesar son of the deified Trajan the Parthian nephew of the deified Nerva Augustus Chief Pontiff holder of his third Tribunician Power thrice Consul ordered the restoration for the city of the Cyrenians of the Baths with the porticos and ballcourts and other adjacent buildings which had been destroyed and burnt in the Jewish revolt." The inscription reads like a state prayer and ends with the operative word *jussit*—he ordered (page 134).

Jerusalem, Aelia Capitolina, Hadrian's reconstruction of Jerusalem, as shown in the 5th century map in the Greek Orthodox church at Madeba in East Jordan. The city has kept the same general plan to this day. Among many identifiable sites may be noted A3 Damascus Gate, still called in Arabic "the Gate of the Pillar" from B3; the pillar set up by Hadrian, long since overthrown, G3 the *cardo maximus*, or main street of the city as it still is, F2 the street in the Tyropoeon, as it still is, C1 Hadrian's Arch (plate 18), D4 the church of the Holy Sepulchre and E5 the Citadel (page 166).

Jerusalem. Hadrian's Arch, now known as the *Ecce Homo*, *left*, looking east, as it was when disclosed in 1858; and *right*, looking west, as it is to-day (page 167).

people, namely themselves, to whom he had revealed his divine will. He had given them a sign of his special relationship with them, circumcision, and he had vouchsafed to them a lawgiver, Moses, and a succession of prophets, by whose preaching their faith had gradually evolved, from being that of a tribal god to an exalted conception of the soul's destiny, which should embrace all mankind. "My House"—the Temple of the Jews—"shall be called a house of prayer for all nations."

Clearly, these two ideas, the Greek and the Jewish, would find it hard to co-exist. The first open breach between them had occurred under the Seleucid king, Antiochus Epiphanes, who, as his cognomen implies, regarded himself as god made manifest. He tried to obliterate Judaism. The Jews replied to his threat by ranging themselves behind a band of brothers called the Maccabees, shaking off the Greek yoke, and establishing a theocratic state, ruled by priest-kings. More than ever the Jews felt themselves to be separate, different, and superior morally to others, as indeed, if they observed the commandments of their God, they were.

For such a polity, Rome could have no use: it must go, and go it did. When, in the hey-day of her eastern expansion under Pompey, Rome came to Judaea, the last of the priest-kings was suppressed, Jerusalem was captured, and the gentile Pompey strode unpunished into the Holy of Holies itself. That was in 63 B.C. The next century saw the grip of Rome gradually tightening over the Jews and their land. At first, by the address of a gifted family of Arab origin but Jewish faith, the Herods, a head-on collision was averted. But after A.D. 6, when Judaea (like other client kingdoms) became a province, things went from bad to worse, with only one tranquil interlude from A.D. 41 to 44, when the client kingdom was revived under Herod Agrippa I. After his untimely death, back came the procurators, with all their gentile paraphernalia, and the fatal train was laid of misunderstanding, provocation and repression which led inevitably to open war. This had started in 66, and the terrible climax had come four years later when, after a siege which recalled that of Carthage, Jerusalem was, like Carthage, destroyed. The Temple had been burned to ashes, and its holy vessels carried off to Rome to grace the triumph of the victor, Titus, on whose memorial arch they may still be seen in effigy.

For the Jews, it might well have seemed the end; but they

could not believe that they, God's people, had been defeated. They continued to hope and to plan.

In this they were greatly helped by the fact that Palestine and Jewry were by no means co-terminous: there were Jewish communities in almost every province, every great city of the empire. Since the days of Julius Caesar, they had lived quietly and peaceably, according to their own laws and customs, among their gentile fellow-subjects. Their privileges had often been re-affirmed. There had been little friction, or persecution, except in one country, and that was Egypt. Alexandria, ever since its foundation by Alexander the Great in the fourth century B.C., had been the hearth and home of Hellenism. It was also the centre of a large Jewish community, who had become so imbued with the Greek atmosphere of the city that they even used a Greek version of their scriptures. Some of their teachers, such as the eminent Philo, went farther, and tried to evolve a system which should reconcile the law of Moses with Greek philosophy.

Unfortunately, both on the Greek and on the Jewish side there were less moderate and peaceful elements, the Jewish extremists being constantly reinforced by emigrants from Palestine, where disturbances became endemic, as they have repeatedly done since. An ugly race riot broke out in A.D. 38—"the first pogrom in Jewish history" in the view of a modern Zionist. A settlement of the dispute was only arrived at in 41 by the emperor Claudius, who, according to the Alexandrine Greeks, was the son of a Jewish mother. He did not favour the Jews. He confirmed them in their rights, but forbade any further immigration, and excluded them from the gymnasium, which meant that they were thus deprived of the secondary education which was the prerequisite to citizenship or to the entering of Greek society and official life. The Jews were to be second-class citizens.

The aftermath of 70 hit the Jews all over the empire, not merely those in Palestine. "The chastisement decided upon by Vespasian," writes Tcherikover, in his lucid *Prolegomena* to Volume I of the *Corpus Papyrorum Judaicorum*, "was a curious mixture of practical financial measures and cynical mockery. The Jews had to pay the *didrachmon*—the half of a shekel, previously paid by every Jew to the Temple of Jerusalem—to the Roman rival of the Jewish God, Jupiter Capitolinus. Since the temple of Jupiter had been burnt down in A.D. 69, the new emperor's first duty was to reconstruct it, and the vanquished nation had to defray the expense. So the *fiscus Judaicus* [Jewish fund, or chest] was founded. Its administrative centre was Rome and it had procurators of its own. The sums due from the Jews were extracted with extreme harshness, especially under Domitian (Suetonius, *Domitian*, 12. 2). Under Nerva the abuses of the exaction were abolished, and the Roman senate even ordered a coin to be struck in order to celebrate this act of liberality. . . . Since it was sufficiently well known that the imposition of this tax was a punitive measure, the Jews were put to shame not only in the eyes of the Greeks but in the eyes of the Egyptian villagers as well. The payment of the Jewish tax acquired something of the significance of the 'yellow spot' on Jews' clothes in the Middle Ages; it marked the Jews as a dangerous and seditious people."

Dangerous and seditious they soon proved themselves.

In the year 115/116, while Trajan was busy with his Parthian campaign, a widespread Jewish revolt broke out. Starting in Egypt, the rebellion spread to Cyrene, where a Messiah, called Loukuas or Andreas, led the insurgents. It involved Cyprus, where the Jews behaved with great ferocity against their Greek neighbours. Alexandria was wrecked, so was Salamis in Cyprus, and so was Cyrene. Its temples were overthrown, and even the road to its seaport, Apollonia, was destroyed. Thousands of Greeks were slaughtered. The inference is that, under Loukuas, or Andreas, the Jews of Cyrene saw themselves as the spearhead of a "Return": they would leave Cyrene for ever, and march back to Palestine, at the head of a victorious legion of their co-religionists in Egypt. The Jews from "beyond the river", that is in Mesopotamia, would join them. A new Zion would arise from the ruins of the old. This outbreak of what was really primitive Zionism took three years to quell. The great Marcius Turbo was despatched to Egypt, where, after killing large numbers of Jews, he restored order. In Mesopotamia the sinister but competent Moor, Lusius Quietus (see page 44), crushed the insurgents, and then became governor of Judaea. In this office he shewed himself so ruthless that in Jewish tradition "the war of Quietus" takes its place between those waged by Vespasian and Hadrian. As a protest against his severity, the Jews abandoned the use of chaplets at betrothal festivals, and gave up teaching their children Greek. More and more they cultivated the nationalist myth, naming their children after the Hebrew patriarchs, and dreamed still of a Messiah who should arise to set his people free and restore Jerusalem. Such was the state of Jewry when Hadrian became emperor.

Meanwhile, an even more puzzling problem from the Roman point of view had arisen in the increase of certain people called Christians. Some said they were a kind of Jew, others that they were a new sect altogether. There was good reason for both views. Everybody knew that they had started in Judaea, and that their founder had been a Jew called Jesus the Christ, or Anointed One, i.e., Messiah. He had become famous throughout the Levant, by his teaching, by the magnetic charm of his personality, by his many acts of healing of mind and body, above all by the flawless beauty and purity of his life. He had told his friends, and indeed any who cared to come and hear him talk as he went up and down the country, that a new epoch was at hand. The Temple was obsolete, Jerusalem was no longer to be the privileged centre of worship. "God is Spirit," he told a woman one day, "and they that worship him must worship him in spirit and in truth"—not in a house made with hands. The established hierarchy, who lived off the Temple, and regarded themselves as the only possible establishment, resented this sort of talk. They contrived to have Jesus arrested and executed by a weak Roman governor, called Pontius Pilate, on the ground that he was a dangerous nationalist. Many people thought this a miscarriage of justice. When, three days after the execution, Jesus appeared again to his intimate friends, there was great consternation. More and more of them were conscious of his presence, and when, after a month or so, that personal presence was taken from them, it was replaced by a spirit of comfort, as Jesus had promised.

At once the new movement, or "way", as those who walked in it preferred to call it, attracted adherents. To start with, these were Jews, including many Essenes, the most spiritually-minded of their people. The Essenes lived a communal life, and for a time the followers of the way did, too. The whole future of the new faith was changed by one of the strangest, strongest characters in history, Paul of Tarsus. From violent opposition to the new way, he became its most eloquent and active advocate; but with one vital modification. Paul realised that not only was patriotism not enough: it was a great deal too much. Jesus, he said, had intended his way to be open to every man, be he Jew or Gentile. This radical departure from orthodoxy shocked many of Jesus' friends; but Paul prevailed.

It is well to remember, when reading the New Testament, that its earliest documents are not the Gospels, although they are placed first, but the epistles of St. Paul: it is from these amazing letters that we gain our knowledge of what the faith was that the apostles proclaimed and the first Christians received, it is from them that we see how quickly and widely it spread and took root —Philippi, Colossæ, Galatia, Corinth, Ephesus, Rome itself. For this there were two main reasons: the first is the genius of Paul. He grasped the central fact that with the coming of Jesus of Nazareth a new epoch had begun. Through the blizzard of opposition he had emerged into the radiance of faith. He could hardly find language in which to express his thoughts and convictions. He knew, as a Jew, how much the new dispensation owed to the old; but as a Roman citizen he knew that Palestine was a Jewish enclave in the most brilliant and living part of the Hellenic world, and that to reach that world he must write in Greek. Even the Greek language, supple and rich as it is, hardly sufficed for the novelty, the revolutionary innovation, of Paul's ideas. To word after word he gave a wholly new signification, words such as those which in our versions are rendered by *repentance, patience, grace, faith, hope, love* and many others. Men and women were suddenly made aware of a new world of spiritual experience, of which the title deeds were theirs.

The second reason was the fact of Jesus himself. Isis, Mithras, Serapis, they sounded attractive, but no one had ever seen them, nor heard them, nor been healed or blessed by them. Thousands, in one of the busiest regions of the world, had known Jesus. He was real and actual. The only surviving fragment of the first Christian apologist makes this very point. It was written by Quadratus, who is said to have presented it to Hadrian in Athens in the year 125. "The works of our Saviour were always present", says Quadratus, quoted by Eusebius (H.E. iv, 3) "for they were genuine: namely those who were healed, those who rose from the dead; who were not only seen in the act of being healed or raised but were also always present; and not merely when the Saviour was on earth, but after his departure as well, they lived for a considerable time, insomuch that some of them survived to our own day." In the Levant the written word has always been secondary, as a means of communication. It is the spoken word that is paramount. The fame of Jesus was the talk of all Syria in no time, and quickly spread beyond its borders.

The new faith was from the outset international, as its Founder had proclaimed that it must be. As recorded in Chapter VII, Judaism had for long attracted a number of the more sensitive souls among the Gentiles; but many others had been deterred by the necessity of submitting to circumcision, and so becoming a member of a defined community. Many Jews, even, who wished to move among Gentiles as one of them, concealed their origin by means of plastic surgery. The new way, while offering all the spiritual nourishment of Judaism, knew no national boundaries. The idea, therefore, that the Christian faith was a sort of underground movement, promoted by slaves lurking in catacombs, must be dismissed as fiction. From the start, its appeal was universal.

Jesus had a friend at the court of Herod Antipas. Herod's foster-brother was an adherent of his way. The faith was early established at Rome. Tacitus mentions Christ, Suetonius the Christians. The Christian apologist Tertullian, writing about 197, says, in a passage of his apology to which too little attention has been paid (but see Sordi, cited in *Sources and Acknowledgments*), that Tiberius, when he received Pontius Pilate's report on the trial and execution of Jesus, wanted to enrol him among the gods of Rome, but that the senate objected on the ground that they knew too little about him. In an apology, a man does not write what is demonstrably false, for one proved error invalidates the whole.

Nero's persecution of the Christians had given them the cachet of status.

But they were elusive, these Christians. What *did* they believe, and who was a Christian? How could one tell? The Jews were at least a recognised and recognisable unit: they lived together, and apart. But the Christians were everywhere. Very early they had organised themselves into Churches. That of Jerusalem was venerated as the mother Church, but in matters of administration the Church of Rome, as that of the capital, had acquired a certain prestige. Thus, it is no surprise to find Clement, a bishop of Rome, writing, about the year 96, to the Church of Corinth on the subject of the ministry.

Not unnaturally, the existence of an organised, international society, dedicated to the worship of a deity other than Caesar, aroused the suspicion of Rome's rulers.

Under Nero, under Domitian, they had faced persecution. Not infrequently, orthodox Jews had contributed to their arrest: in the early days of the new faith there was a period of polemic between Jew and Christian, of which snatches may be gleamed from the Talmud (e.g., *Aboda Zara* 17a), without there being a complete break. They bandy texts, rather as Catholic and Protestant used to do. The Jewish attempt to "frame" the so-called "brethren of the Lord", told of in Eusebius, III, 20, is part of this controversy. They were delated, says the historian, by the Jews for claiming royal descent. This was clever, for if they had maintained their claim, the Romans would have been very suspicious of them, while if they denied it, the Christians preaching of the "new kingdom" would be discredited in the eyes of all Jews.

Ignatius of Antioch—the city, capital of the east, in which the followers of Christ were first called Christians—had suffered public martyrdom in Rome in the days of Trajan, whose attitude to Christianity was equivocal, typical of the puzzled incomprehension and suspicion which that religion aroused. In Bithynia, that sensitive province in which even a fire brigade was rightly regarded as a potential focus of sedition, Pliny, when governor in the year 111 or 112 had come up against the problem. He wrote a long letter to Trajan asking for guidance. He was not sure, he said, whether the Christians should be punished simply for being Christians, or whether for the "secret crimes" connected with the name. His procedure was to call the accused into court, and bid them recite a prayer to the gods at his dictation, venerate the statue of the emperor and curse Christ. Those who refused he sent to execution. From apostates he had gathered that the Christians, on a fixed day, held a service before dawn and took an oath, not to commit crimes, but the very reverse, to abstain from crime, and to keep faith with all men. To test this assertion, Pliny had two deaconesses tortured, but could discover "nothing else than a perverse and extravagant superstition". It was disturbing, he said, because it was spreading among people of all ranks, in town and country alike. On the other hand, there did seem to be a revival of traditional temple-worship, and if the right steps were taken now, it ought to be possible to stamp the new superstition out. Pliny had evidently started from the simple assumption that to be a Christian was enough cause for death, but had wavered when he found out how widespread the faith had become, and how blameless its adherents were.

Trajan's reply is one of the most famous letters in history:

"You have adopted the proper course, my dear Secundus [i.e., Pliny], in your examination of the cases of those who were accused to you as Christians, for indeed nothing can be laid down as a general ruling involving something like a set form of procedure. They are not to be sought out; but if they are accused and convicted, they must be punished—yet on this condition, that whosoever denies himself to be a Christian, and makes the fact plain by his action, that is by worshipping our gods, shall obtain pardon on his repentance, however suspicious his past conduct may be. Papers, however, which are presented unsigned ought not to be admitted in any charge [Pliny had confessed to having acted partly on anonymous information], for they are a very bad example and unworthy of our time."

This letter came under Tertullian's lash within the century. "What a decision, how inevitably entangled! He says they must not be sought out, implying they are innocent, and he orders them to be punished, implying they are guilty. He spares them and rages against them, he pretends not to see, and punishes." In d'Orgeval's words, "By this letter, the conqueror of Dacia and Parthia puts himself at a distance from Alexander to draw nearer to Pontius Pilate." There was, all the same, a good deal of sense in Trajan's decision. It avoided constant difficulties such as Pliny had been faced with, but reserved a sanction which could be imposed if necessary.

Hadrian's policy was very much the same as Trajan's—for which this time Tertullian among other Christian writers was to commend him. A governor of Asia called Granianus had written to Hadrian about the Christian problem. Unfortunately we do not possess his letter. But we have Hadrian's letter to his successor, Fundanus, written, it is said, after Quadratus and two other prominent Christians had interceded with the emperor, in the year 125: "I have received the letter written to me by your predecessor, the most illustrious Serenius Granianus, and it is not my pleasure to pass by without inquiry the matter referred to me lest both the innocent should be disturbed and an opportunity of plunder afforded to slanderous informers. Now, if our subjects of the provinces are able to sustain by evidence this their petition against the Christians, so as to accuse them before a Court of Justice, I have no objection to their taking this course. But I do not allow them to use mere clamorous demands and outcries for this purpose. For it is much more equitable, if any one wishes to accuse them, for you to take cognizance of the matters laid to their charge. If therefore anyone accuses and proves that the aforesaid men do anything contrary to the laws, you will also determine their punishments in accordance with their offences. You will on the other hand, by Hercules, take particular care that if any one demand a writ of accusation against any of these Christians, merely for the sake of libelling them, you proceed against that man with heavier penalties in accordance with his heinous guilt" (tr. J. Stevenson in *A New Eusebius*).

Stevenson comments: "The increase in numbers and popularity of a religious sect which did not afford reciprocal toleration to the pagan deities, and was (unlike the Jews) international, caused the pagans to raise tumults against them, particularly in times of public stress . . . It is clear that the emperor preserves the principle laid down by Trajan; nothing was to be allowed against the Christians except on regular accusation."

Justin, a contemporary apologist, regards this rescript as securing the Christians against persecution, as does also Melito of Sardis, in the days of Marcus Aurelius, who makes it clear that Hadrian's policy, as given in his letter to Fundanus, was of general application: "Your grandfather Hadrian wrote to the proconsul Fundanus, governor of Asia, as well as to many others besides . . . that they should raise no disturbances concerning us." Hadrian was later even believed, wrongly, to have built churches, partly because his own temples were devoid of images and partly, no doubt, because of the hostility he had shewn to the Jews. Even the pagan authors of the *Augustan History* say, rather vaguely, that Hadrian "thought of" building churches.

From the foregoing, it will be seen that already, by the days of Hadrian, the outlook for the Christians, although they still had trials to undergo, was much brighter than it was for the Jews. Jesus had turned the direction of life, its moral goal, from the nation, that is his own Jewish nation, to the individual soul, which has no nationality. From Paul to Pasternak, men of Jewish race have besought their brother Jews to heed the message. In Hadrian's day, as in later ages, their tragic inability to do so was to bring upon them unspeakable calamity.

Chapter XIX

O JERUSALEM, JERUSALEM!

"THE inspection of the troops stationed in Palestine was not the least important reason which brought the emperor to that country. Nothing better demonstrates the care which Hadrian took of the military situation than the number of coins which were struck in connexion with his journeys, bearing on the obverse the designations of the different army corps, drawn from the names of the countries they occupied, with the portrait of the emperor addressing the troops which made up the garrison. That is how we learn that in the east he visited the armies known respectively as the Cappadocian, the Parthian, the Syrian and the Judaean. This last, in the year 86, comprised two legions, two wings and four cohorts. In the year 130 it must have been the same. Two detachments, one from the Xth, Straits, the other from the VIth, Ironclads, bear witness (in inscriptions) that they had worked on the aqueduct at Caesarea in the name of Hadrian Augustus." Thus does Abel (Volume II, page 80) introduce Hadrian to the Holy Land. He came primarily as a soldier. His idea of naming the armies after the provinces in which they served was part and parcel of his partnership policy. But it was not popular with the conservatives, who liked to think of the great Roman army, the iron hand of the Quirites, as a single mighty instrument. From the practical point of view, apart from the political aspect, Hadrian was right, because the army was no longer Roman or even predominantly Italian in composition. Only the Guard remained Italian.

Palestine has seen as many armies as any country in all the world. But it is also the land where, in the words of an old Jewish priest, "the day-spring from on high hath visited us, to give light to them that sit in darkness and in the shadow of death, and to guide our feet into the way of peace" (Luke 1, 78-9). When Hadrian arrived in Jerusalem, the Temple in which these words had been uttered over a hundred and thirty years before was a mound of rubble. By the time Titus had captured the city in A.D.

70, it had been almost completely destroyed. No doubt Josephus—our only contemporary source for this catastrophe—did not minimise the destruction, first, because the victor was his patron; secondly, because the object of his book was to deter others, specially his Jewish brethren, from undertaking a similar disastrous revolt. Even he admits that a part of the great upper citadel was left standing, as a memorial of Titus' valour. It still stands: the truth is that it is practically indestructible. But there were also other parts of the city which had either escaped destruction, or on the ruins of which little "shanty-towns" had grown up. In the first place there was a legion stationed in the citadel, and so, as invariably happens, a commercial suburb sprang up round it. Eusebius, the fourth-century historian, says that half the city had escaped destruction. St. Epiphanius (315-403), who, though he became archbishop of Cyprus, was, like Eusebius, a Palestinian, says that in Hadrian's day Jerusalem housed not only the church of the Christians who had returned from Trans-Jordan after A.D. 70, but no less than seven synagogues, for Jews were not yet forbidden access to their city. Rabbinical literature supports him. A certain Rabbi Eleazar, who had survived the siege, lays down rules for shopkeepers who have to deal with non-Jewish clients. The Fourth Book of Esdras, and the Pseudo-Baruch who set himself up in a cave in the Kedron valley, undertook to raise the spirits of the faithful, and to keep alive their hope for an eventual restoration.

How would the Jews receive Hadrian? They had, it is true, much cause to suspect his intentions. Nevertheless, they would give him a trial. The inhabitants of Palestine always hope that a new régime will be better than that under which they live, that the devil they don't know will be better than the devil they do. So far, they have almost always been disappointed. Hadrian had, after all, executed the terrible Quietus. He had also, if we are to believe a fragment from the works of Hippolytus, a third-century schismatic bishop of Rome, authorised the removal of Trajan's statue from the Holy Mountain, the site of the Temple. Jewish tradition goes even further. Hadrian, they said, really intended to rebuild their Temple, and it was only the intrigues of the Judeao-Christians and the Samaritans that dissuaded him. Poor hopeful Jews! They were soon to learn the truth.

As we have already seen, Hadrian saw himself as another

Antiochus Epiphanes. He was soon to prove it. The Jews, he now realised, were impostors. Who ever had heard of a religion without a temple? Where theirs had been, for two generations nothing had stood—the site was just a hill like any other, on which Trajan's statue had been placed, as on scores of other hills all over the empire. But what a superb site it was! Clearly, it called for replanning. It would not be the first new city he had begotten, nor the last, if he could help it. If, up in Galilee, the Greek inhabitants of Tiberias could honour him, as they had done, despite the opposition of their Jewish fellow-citizens, with a temple, why should not he build on the ruins of Jerusalem a fine new city, with a temple dedicated to his own cult? What should it be called? Hadrianopolis, like the rest? No, not here. Among these stiff-necked Semites, it was *Rome* that must be proclaimed. The new city must be an imperial lighthouse and fortress. So it must have a Roman name, the names of Rome's emperor and Rome's capitol. *Aelia* (Hadrian's patronymic) *Capitolina*, it should be called. Jerusalem was to be obliterated—not only physically but even as a memory. The actual plan of Hadrian's creation, which has lasted to our own day, will be discussed in Chapter XXI.

Yet another blow was to be struck at these dissidents, these nonconformists. Hadrian forbade circumcision. Anyone who practised it was to suffer the penalty for castration, which was death. This decree was aimed not only against the Jews, but against all the peoples, and they were many in the Levant and Africa, who circumcised their children as their fathers had done before them. That the decree was universal we know from the fact that the Jews, with that obstinacy which has so often been their most unpopular and serviceable weapon, obtained from the emperor Antoninus, Hadrian's successor, a revocation of the edict for themselves only. For the rest, it was a nuisance: only for the Jews a sacrilege. The command can never have been carried out with anything like general obedience. Why did Hadrian try to impose it? There were two reasons. First, with all his liberality of mind, all his longing to see the empire as a company of equal provinces, he envisaged them as a Roman society, a coherent society. There was no room, in his theory, for any "opting-out", any separatism, and what could be more separatist than this bodily mark? In an age when physical exercise and washing were habitually carried out naked and in company, nothing could be more blatant. Secondly, Hadrian was a Hellenist. To the Greek, man was the measure of all things, mind and body. To dare to modify that body, in any detail at all, was to the Greek a blasphemy. Seen in this light, Hadrian's decree is understandable, even though its results, in the case of the Jews, only served to make a bad state of affairs worse.

Having given his orders for the design and construction of Aelia Capitolina, Hadrian moved south. He was bent on visiting Egypt, where he had never been. He was bound, as every Jew in Palestine knew, for Alexandria, to hobnob with, and to flatter, those Greeks who had shewn themselves such enemies to the Jews. On the way, as if to leave no one in doubt of his attitude, he halted, just short of Pelusium, and erected a monument over the funeral mound of Pompey the Great, who had been murdered as he landed on the Egyptian strand after his defeat by Julius Caesar, and who had for 178 years lain there unhonoured. "Hardly a tomb he had, who was so rich in temples", in the words of the epitaph which Hadrian recited, and probably composed. As we have seen, Hadrian the antiquarian delighted in restoring the sepulchres of bygone heroes—Ajax, Alcibiades, Epameinondas and now Pompey, who, although he had been the rival, and the defeated rival, of Julius Caesar, the "father" of Augustus, the Great Model, was nevertheless revered, and rightly revered, as a great Roman. Hadrian's action in granting him at last a decent resting-place was like the action of King George IV in commissioning Canova to fashion the memorial in St. Peter's, Rome, to the last Stewarts, in which they are given the royal titles to which they pretended. It was a large-hearted gesture. But what an effect it must have had on the Jews!

Here, in summary, are the grievances which by the year 130 the Jews had, or imagined they had—for, as in all such cases, certainty was barnacled with suspicion—against Hadrian. First, he had declared himself the successor of Antiochus Epiphanes. He had finished Antiochus' own temple in Athens. Secondly, like Antiochus, he had adopted, or allowed others to adopt in addressing him, the style of god, of Zeus Olympios. Thirdly, he had permitted this style to appear on coins which circulated among Jewish communities. Fourthly, he had prohibited circumcision, which for the Jews was the very seal of their being and faith. Fifthly, he was on his way to patronise and caress the Greeks of Alexandria, who had shewn themselves the most ardent enemies of the Jews. Sixthly, he had gone out of his way to honour the very man who had captured Jerusalem, almost two centuries before, and had violated the Holy of Holies. Seventhly, and finally, he had given orders for the obliteration of Jerusalem, for the construction on the site of a Roman colony, called by his own name, and containing, on the very site of the ancient Temple, a shrine where he himself should be venerated.

It was a formidable catalogue. Before the year was out, Hadrian was to add yet an eighth count: the deification of his favourite. There was, as there always is, the other side. Pausanias says that Hadrian never provoked a war, and only waged it when forced. The instigators were the nationalists, the extremists who could not see that conformity, acceptance of Rome's enlightened and benignant rule, was best for all concerned. The situation, the cross-purposed misunderstanding, has recurred in later ages, within other empires. Here was its first tragic example. Given the Jews' conviction, whether justified or not, that they were a separate and superior people, that the destruction of their Temple was a mere temporary disaster—were not its very measurements, together with every detail of its ritual, preserved in the archives that later became the Mishnah?—it is hardly to be wondered at that they longed, as of old, for a Judas Maccabaeus.

To their undying misfortune, they were to find one.

Chapter XX

"IN MY END IS MY BEGINNING"

IN no city of the empire was Hadrian assured of a warmer welcome than in Alexandria. For one thing, it was a Greek creation, the capital which Alexander the Great had founded, and in which the first Ptolemy had buried Alexander's corpse, after high-jacking it on its way from Babylon. Succeeding Ptolemies had raised the city to the height of splendour and influence. It possessed an unrivalled library, its Museum might claim to be the prototype of the modern university, its palaces, temples and colonnades reflected the bright sun by day and the sheen of torches by night, for Alexandria even had street-lighting. The city was also very rich, being the centre of the Egyptian corn-trade, and the terminal of the vastly lucrative eastern traffic, of which mention has already been made.

The town had suffered disastrously during the Jewish rising fifteen years before. It was ironical that in the very city where Philo and his like had striven so earnestly and sincerely to discover a basis for the co-existence of Jew with Gentile, the poison injected by refugee terrorists from Palestine, after the First Revolt, should have ended in the extermination of the whole of Alexandrine Jewry. For that was the result. The Jews fought with the ferocity of fanaticism against their gentile neighbours. They wrecked Alexandria. When at last Turbo had restored order, after killing multitudes of Jews, Hadrian expelled the rest and ordered the rebuilding of the city. He was now greeted as its saviour and founder. Hadrian was in his element, disputing with the professors of the university, some at least of whom he had, as we have seen, himself appointed.

It seems probable that it was on this occasion that Hadrian visited Cyrene, which, like Alexandria, had suffered such ruination during the Jewish revolt, of which, indeed, it seems to have been the centre. Weber would have had the emperor include Cyrene in his "African" tour of 122; but to this there are two objections. The first is that Cyrenaica is territorially linked with

Egypt, and cut off from "Africa" by the Gulf of Sirte, which, as anyone who has wandered in that region knows, is one of the world's great natural barriers. The second is that, supposing Hadrian to have made the journey by ship, it is unlikely that he should not then have gone on to Alexandria where, in 122 as later, there were pressing problems to be solved. At this length of time, the exact date of Hadrian's visit is not of prime importance—if, indeed, he ever did visit it, for we have no absolutely conclusive evidence: what makes Cyrene so significant to the modern student of Hadrian is that it affords as good an example as any, better even than Athens and Jerash, of how Hadrian could re-found a Greek city, and infuse into it his own Hellenism.

Cyrene was the first Greek colony to be planted in the continent of Africa. That was in the seventh century B.C. It lasted right down to Byzantine days, more than a millennium, longer than the republic of Venice. The site is superb, recalling that of Thera, or Santorin, the island from which its founders came— a throne of tree-clad limestone, two and a half thousand feet high, between the Mediterranean, to which it is joined by two steps, as it were, and the boundless desert to the south. "It is hard to believe," says Mr. R. D. Barnett, "when one is standing in this earthly paradise that one is standing in Africa at all." If ever, for a Greek, there was a home from Hellas, it is Cyrene. From Cyrene Hellenism quickly radiated all over the "Green Mountain"—to Barce, on whose plum-coloured plain, where a later generation was to hunt the fox, the Greeks invented four-horse chariot-racing; to Apollonia, on the coast below, to Ptolemais (Tolmeita), to Berenice (Benghazi) to Teuchira (Tocra). Its spring was soon sanctified to Apollo, in whose honour a shrine arose. Zeus was honoured with a temple in the Doric style, erected ten years before the Parthenon, and the only Doric temple in Africa. It was, naturally, to the sea, and to Hellas, that this lonely outpost on a foreign shore for ever looked. It exported its grain and its famous silphium to Greek cities. Its roses were renowned, its olive oil was said to give a brighter flame than any other. From the south it attracted gold, gems, ostrich feathers, salt. Its horses were celebrated. So were its scholars and poets. Plato himself had a Cyrenaican mathematics teacher, and it was a Cyrenian who ransomed him from the slave market at Aegina.

Rome had acquired Cyrene by the "bequest" of its last Greek

Rome. The obelisk erected by Hadrian as a memorial to
Antinoüs, now on the Pincio (page 156).

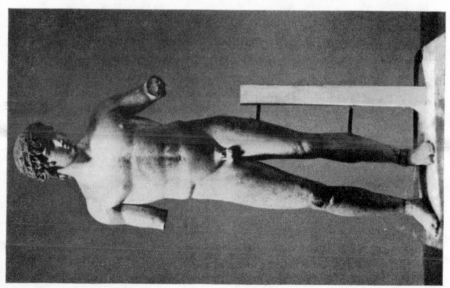

Antinoüs. *Left,* the statue in the Delphi Museum; *right,* that in the Olympia Museum. It is possible that both these statues were done from life (*page 92*)

Antinoüs. The "Braschi" statue in the Vatican, shewing Antinoüs as Dionysus. "For almost the first time since the fourth century a type of physical beauty is taken from a real head and not from a copy-book. . . . The physical character of Antinoüs is still perceptible when, after its long banishment, the Apollonian nude returns in the person of Donatello's David." Sir K. Clark, *The Nude*. Lord Tennyson, gazing at a statue of Antinoüs in the British Museum, is recorded by Edmund Gosse to have exclaimed: "The inscrutable Bithynian. . . . If we knew what he knew, we should understand the ancient world."

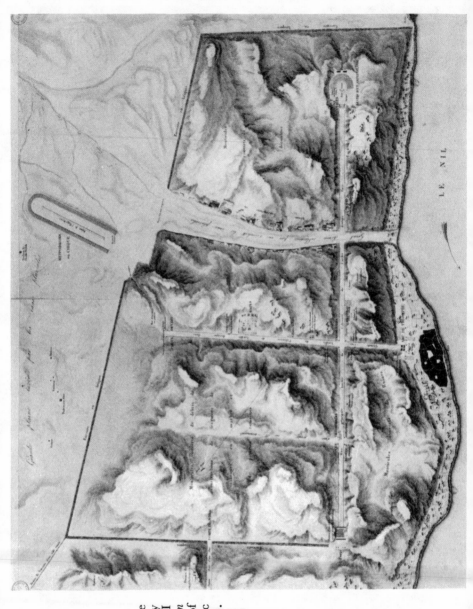

LE NIL

Antinoöpolis. The beautiful plan given by Jomard in Volume VI of his *Déscription d'Egypte*, the fruit of Napoleon's scientific expedition (page 156).

ruler in 96 B.C. By the days of Augustus it had attracted a large Jewish community, one of whom, called Simon, was to achieve immortality as the bearer of Christ's cross. As in Alexandria, the Jews were guaranteed their traditional privileges, including that of sending tribute to the Temple in Jerusalem, but were excluded from the *palaestra*, and so from the civil service and the administration. (They were treated, in fact, as Roman Catholics were for so long treated in England and Ireland.)

Cyrene was, like Alexandria, wrecked in the rising of 115/116, and was then restored by Hadrian's orders. The magnificent range of buildings which, thanks to the labours of Italian and American archaeologists, we can contemplate today, is therefore almost wholly of Hadrian's creation. The temples of Apollo, Artemis, the new temple of Hecate, the Capitolium, that is the temple of Jupiter, Juno and Minerva, the gods of the Roman Capitol, now newly built, the shrine of Caesar—all of these grand relics bear inscriptions praising Hadrian as their restorer. The emperor also restored the baths, as a beautifully inscribed and most Roman inscription records (see Plate 16). The baths—and surely the emperor himself saw to this?—were now divided into two sections, the greater baths with statues and mosaics, for the men, the lesser for the women, and, as we can see by the graded latrines, for the little children, too. Hadrian also founded a new town on the coast between Berenice and Teuchira, called Hadriana (Driana), which today is no more than a deserted mound. But of all the monuments to Hadrian which we still possess, Cyrene has a unique appeal, because from Cyrene we can judge of the rejuvenation which Hadrian brought to many another ancient city throughout the empire.

We must now return, with Hadrian, to Egypt.

For such a mind as Hadrian's, so sensitive, so enquiring, a mere visit to Alexandria, delightful as it was, was not enough. He must see Egypt as well, and that, for him, as for us, meant a trip up the Nile. Two centuries before, Julius Caesar had taken one with Cleopatra; but since then, none of Rome's rulers had ever seen at first hand the country on which Rome depended for its very existence; for it was from Egypt that the greater part of Rome's grain supply was shipped. When, after the defeat of Antony and Cleopatra in 31 B.C., Egypt fell to the victor, Augustus, with the business acumen he had inherited from his banking ancestors, at once realised that so valuable an asset must be kept secure at all costs: it must never become a political pawn, nor the base of a possible rival. He therefore kept Egypt entirely outside the provincial framework of the empire. It was his personal appanage, governed by a prefect appointed by him. Nor might anyone of consular rank even visit Egypt without a special visa from the emperor. How far-sighted Augustus was, was proved in the year 69, when Vespasian, by establishing himself in Egypt, in a position to starve Rome into submission, made certain his elevation to the purple.

Egypt, although it fronts the Mediterranean, is not a Mediterranean country. Egypt is African. Nowhere in Egypt are to be found the limestone terraces clothed with olive and carob, the tawny-red soil, the vineyards and the cornfields, nourished by the former and the latter rains, which make up the eternal harmony, the never-ending cycle of life around the inland sea. Egypt knows none of this simple self-contained beauty. The life of Egypt is based on extraneous miracle. Its barren sands seem dedicated to death, and yet, through the operation of one single mysterious stream, they yield life abundantly. The Nile, coming no man knew whence, rising year by year, to embrace and fertilise the hungry fields, this god-river *was* Egypt. Juvenal, in a famous line, had complained that long since the Orontes, the river of Syria, had flowed into the Tiber. In truth, for Rome, the Nile was more vital than either Orontes or Tiber.

Nowhere is the physical contrast, the staggering difference, between life and death more actually prominent, more inescapable, than in Egypt, where it is possible, quite literally, to stand with one foot in the desert and the other in the sown. It is small wonder, therefore, that from time immemorial Egypt had been the womb of religion. Those vast temples, those deep-dug tombs, those avenues of unsmiling sphinxes, all that ponderous apparatus of numinosity which strikes awe into the modern traveller, how much more awful must it have been when the gods it served still inhabited it, when Isis and Osiris and Serapis were still acclaimed by thousands of believing votaries, not only in Egypt, but far beyond its bounds? So powerful were they that they mastered even the Greeks themselves. The very Ptolemies, as we learn from their monuments at Karnak, adopted perforce the Egyptian mode, in their architecture, their language, even in their morals,

In Egypt, religion was the ruling passion and was to remain so for centuries to come. That was the Egypt which Hadrian now set out to explore. With him went Sabina (who had joined the emperor at Alexandria, probably), accompanied by a blue-stocking crony called Balbilla. With him, too, went Antinoüs. Southward the party glided on, enjoying the tranquil winter sunshine, and the contemplation of activity they were not called upon to share.

Then, on the 30th October, Antinoüs was drowned. The inquest on his death, the longest and least conclusive inquest in history, is still going on. There are three possible causes of death, misadventure, murder or suicide. The first, for anyone occupying Antinoüs' favoured position, is very unlikely. Wherever he went he would be accompanied by servants and guards. Murder is just possible. "A favourite has no friend", and yet what little we know about Antinoüs, apart from his overpowering beauty, leads us to suppose that he was a modest and intelligent lad. This leaves suicide as the most probable cause. Suicide was, in fact, the answer which men gave in antiquity: what divided opinions was the reason for the suicide. Antinoüs' beauty, taken in conjunction with Hadrian's known liking for males, was made the basis for the foul suggestion that Antinoüs had committed suicide out of shame for a sullied life. Hadrian had many enemies, not only in Rome, but in the provinces, too, where his ruthless punishment of inefficient and corrupt officials had turned many against him: they could now take a nasty, whispered revenge. Many others, throughout history, have followed them. Lucian, the raffish Syrian novelist, uses the word "Bithynian" in a context where it can only be a euphemism for something vile. Julian the Apostate, with shoddy wit, described in his *Caesars* the arrival of Hadrian in heaven. He asks for Antinoüs, whereupon the drunken Silenus roars out: "Looking for Antinoüs? Tell him, someone, to come off it: he won't find the boy here." The Christian Fathers, to whom, as to the Jews, the deification of any human being was an outrage, were as unkind to Hadrian and his reputation as the pagan emperor was, though one of the acutest and fairest of them, the great Origen, writing about a century and a half after the event, accuses Antinoüs of being elevated to renown "by Egyptian magic and spells" merely, and asks "what is there in common between the noble life of our Jesus and the life of the favourite of Hadrian who did not even keep the man from a morbid lust for women?"

155

(*Against Celsus*, III, 36). Down to our own day, there have never been lacking those who hold that the relationship between Hadrian and Antinoüs was an improper one. They even pick on the word *muliebriter*, literally "like a woman", the adverb which his biographer uses to describe how Hadrian cried over his lost friend; whereas it is twice used by Tacitus, in his biography of his father-in-law, in contexts that cannot possibly have any sensual connotation—the word had simply become the stock qualification for violent tears.

Considered calmly, all the evidence points in the other direction.

First, Hadrian was now in his fifties. He was childless, because his unnatural wife boasted that she would never run the risk of giving him any: she had seen to that. It was only natural that Hadrian should desire to adopt some youth who would be as a son to him. Antinoüs was the ideal candidate, gay, intelligent, young, surpassingly handsome. But adopt him Hadrian could not: he knew that he would not nominate an obscure Bithynian, however charming, as his successor in the principate. Antinoüs could nevertheless receive a father's devotion, and return it with a son's affection. On no other reckoning is it in any way possible to explain the posthumous veneration of Antinoüs. He was said to have appeared in the heavens as a new star, and Hadrian was laughed at for believing the tale. But the deification of Antinoüs went ahead. His likeness was venerated throughout the whole empire, often assimilated to Hermes, Apollo, Osiris, Dionysus or to other deities. Orators and poets lauded the dead boy. Antinoüs-games were instituted in Athens, Argos, Eleusis. At Mantineia, the city from which the people of Bithynion claimed that their founders had sprung, Hadrian founded an oracle of Antinoüs, with yearly celebrations, and every fifth year a special festival. A cenotaph (possibly even the actual tomb) of Antinoüs arose in Rome itself (see Plate 19). In Egypt, on the spot near which he was drowned, Hadrian built a whole city, called Antinoöpolis, made it the capital of the region, and tried to divert to it part of the Red Sea trade. This city was not solely designed as a memorial, but as a political buttress to the "presence" of Hellenism in Egypt. It has disappeared, but fortunately enough was still left of it a century and a half ago for Napoleon's savants to survey and describe it (see Plate 22).

Now is it possible that all these manifold commemorations

were so eagerly, so speedily, and so universally, proffered and accepted in honour of a catamite?

Ancient society was corrupt, and both Greek and Roman morals were corroded with pederasty. But there were some things that neither Greece nor Rome would tolerate. It was Nero's lewd ostentation of his vicious passion for Sporus which had brought him to his death, Dion Chrysostom maintained. Hadrian, whatever may have been his private tastes, would be the last to flaunt a connexion of this sort, nor would Rome (which already had little love for him) have tolerated him had he done so. The very monument which commemorates Antinoüs in Rome is a *family* monument, it bears the effigies of Hadrian, Antinoüs, and Sabina, who is never recorded to have spoken or acted against the boy.

Why then did Antinoüs commit suicide? Hadrian's own account—it is one of the very few quotations we have from his autobiography—is that the boy "fell into the Nile"; but the hostile chronicler, after quoting this, immediately says that he sacrificed himself to save Hadrian from some calamity. Hadrian, as we know, was pathologically superstitious. In the awesome, oppressive ambience of destiny which in the Egypt of his day must have been almost overwhelming, the emperor would have been more than ever susceptible and apprehensive. Antinoüs must have known this. Besides, as we know from Epiphanius, Hadrian was already ailing when he set out for Egypt. "All the doctors of the empire had been summoned to cure him, but all to no effect." Antinoüs must have known this, too.

It was held in ancient Egypt that a person who was drowned in the Nile was deified. Of this belief there is evidence as early as the thirteenth dynasty. The honorific of such persons was *Hsy*. Tertullian, in his treatise on baptism, vouches for it: "nam et esittos vocant quos aquae necaverunt"—"they call those whom the waters have killed *Hsy*" (he got as near as his Latin could to the unfamiliar Egyptian word).

Antinoüs resolved to save his beloved emperor. This world, in which the emperor's love had raised him so high, held nothing higher for him. But to become a god, and as the reward for saving the life of Hadrian, what more perfect climax could crown his life? He chose that path: he achieved his deification. In his end was his beginning.

Chapter XXI

JERUSALEM DUSK

PRIVATE sorrow must not interfere with public duty: the party continued its tour as planned. For the emperor, the vivifying Nile was now the river of death; but for his callous empress and the awful Balbilla, it was the path to Thebes, to exciting amusement. To these silly women, the grandeur of antiquity made little appeal: what they wanted to visit was the "singing statue". On the left bank of the Nile, just where the sown gives way to the desert on the road that leads to the Valley of the Kings, stood, and still stand, two colossal statues, known as the Colossi of Memnon, in reality of Amenophis II (1442-1416 B.C.). Both were originally granite monoliths, but the northern one had been broken, either by an earthquake or by the mad Persian king, Cambyses, and its upper portion restored with dressed stones. The statues face the dawn. As the rising sun warmed the northern one, that is about two hours after sunrise, to judge by inscriptions, the expansion of the stone caused the statue to give forth a griding noise "like the snapping of a taut harpstring". By Hadrian's day, this had become a tourist attraction. The royal party twice visited the statue, and heard it "sing". Balbilla recorded the happy event in five dreadful little elegiac poems, in the Aeolic dialect, which she had engraved on the left foot of the statue, that being the established mode even in those days.

The god, says her scrannel ditty, greeted Hadrian before sunrise (which was impossible), again at the second hour and even at the third. Hadrian returned the greeting, and everyone could see how dear he was to the gods. One doubts, though, whether Balbilla was very dear to Hadrian.

Hadrian's visit must have given a stimulus to the tourist traffic, for of the inscriptions scratched on Memnon's left foot (all of which may be examined by the curious in the copper-plates of Richard Pococke's first-hand *Description of the East*, published in 1743), ranging from the time of Nero to that of Caracalla, no less than twenty-seven are of the reign of Hadrian.

The flotilla then turned north, to be borne on the lackeying stream back to the Delta, passing in its course the fatal reach in which Antinoüs had been drowned, and the site where his memorial city was to arise. This took six years to build. It was laid out on the usual plan, and it was adorned with a theatre and temples. It was modelled on Athens, with a population organised in demes and tribes, named after Hadrian, Athena, Aelius, Matidius and so on. Vestiges of the city lasted down to the beginning of the nineteenth century, when they were surveyed by Napoleon's savants (see Plate 22). But decay set in soon afterwards. James Silk Buckingham in 1814 "passed a whole day amid these ruins, which have all the grandeur of Roman times, the architecture being chiefly Corinthian". Eight years later, Robert Richardson reports that "the rows of columns are still standing on each side of the street, some of them are shell-like stone, and others of granite. On the west, or end nearest the river, they begin at a handsome triumphal arch of the Corinthian order, which the inhabitants are pulling down by the order of the governor, and terminate in the east in the remains of an elegant gateway." He adds that the present village was called *Ansine*: the name had survived, although the cult of Antinoüs had long ago fallen into oblivion. It is remarkable that it should have survived as long as it did, well into the fourth century. By 1879, when Villiers Stuart visited the site, all was desolation; no trace of the town remained. Ironically enough, all that now survives is the temple of Rameses, which had stood there for almost two thousand years before Antinoüs was born.

The first months of the year 131 were spent in Alexandria, or near it (was it perhaps during this spring that Hadrian visited Cyrene?). Then in the autumn, he set sail for Syria. Thence he went to Pontus, and his beloved Greece, and was still there when the serious situation in Palestine called him back to that country, where the Jews had now begun their last desperate rebellion.

"Scarcely," says Abel, "had the buildings of Aelia started to rise from the ground, when their construction had to be interrupted. The fire of rebellion, which smouldered beneath its ashes, burst into flames as soon as it was known that the emperor had reached the farthest parts of Asia Minor. Sixty years of slavery since the destruction of the Temple! Was the period of eclipse to be prolonged beyond that of the Babylonian captivity? During this interval, had not the fertility of the race easily succeeded in more than filling the gaps left by former wars? Moreover, the Roman peace which Hadrian boasted that he was consolidating from one end of the empire to the other encroached upon the designs of a people who believed themselves called by God not merely to independence, but to universal sovereignty. There was not lacking a man to give to this new movement a Messianic quality. He is known by his patronymic of Ben or Bar Koziba in Rabbinical literature, but the people, it appears, willingly adopted the paronomasia of *Bar-Kokhba*, put about by the authority of the greatest doctor of the contemporary Synagogue, Rabbi Akiba, who saw in him the Star (*kokab*) which should come out of Jacob, according to the oracle of Balaam (Numbers XXIV, 17). It is under the name of Bar Kokhba, *Son of the Star*, that he is known to Christian writers, ready enough to shew thereby the vanity of a Messianic quality which was belied by events."

It is easy to talk about nationalism, which is often but the patriotism of people we do not like. There have been noble nationalists. The noblest of whom we have record, Robert E. Lee, is himself a case to point the utter irrationality of the nationalist compulsion. At the outbreak of the War between the States, Lee held a commission in the United States army. He did not believe in the right of states to secede from the Union, nor in slavery, the two *casus belli*; but "I am a Virginian"—and so he must fight for the Confederate South, instead of commanding the Federal armies, as he well might have done. The decision of this one great man, this noble and devout Virginian, gives an air of fatal futility to the whole of that disastrous war. Yet, today, a century later, Lee is venerated almost as a saint in the state of his birth. Secondly, although in our own day nationalism is out of date, so that nationalists arouse pity rather than scorn, far less admiration, it is well to remember that not so long ago, even the English were nationalists, proclaiming their divine and chosen destiny with a more than Jewish conviction. In short, no nationalism, no nation: no nation, no internationalism.

But, however liberal and indulgent a view we may adopt towards nationalism in the round, the Jewish revolt of the year 132 cannot enlist our active sympathy, for two reasons. First, it

The Palestrina mosaic, shewing Egypt as it was in Hadrian's day. At the bottom is Alexandria, the capital, with an official gathering. Other details shew temples, villas, cottages, boats and, at the top, hunting scenes in the Sudan (page 154).

Ostia. This picture gives some idea of the spacious and airy new town designed and built under Hadrian's direction (page 168).

Hadrian's Villa. The small baths. The growth of the Roman vault may here be studied. No Gothic vault ever equalled it in its grandest expression. The span of the largest existing Gothic vault, in the cathedral of Gerona, is 73 feet, a figure exceeded in the basilica of Maxentius and the imperial Baths in Rome. The throne-room of Domitian had a clear span of about 100 feet. The widest Gothic vault in England, Ely Cathedral Lady Chapel, is only 46 feet.

could not possibly succeed. Terrorism can prove fruitful only in a liberal atmosphere. Ireland, India, Morocco, Palestine—to quote but four modern examples—have all experienced successful campaigns of "rebel" violence, which, by their effect on liberal opinion in the world at large, have been the prelude to political success. But against a Rome or a Russia such methods must always be useless. The second reason is the personality of Bar Kokhba, a narrow, selfish fanatic. One of his uncles, we know, came from Modin, the village of the Maccabees, and Bar Kokhba no doubt saw himself in the dual rôle of Maccabee and Messiah. Rebel movements generally enlist the patronage of a prelate: Akiba gave his blessing to Bar Kokhba. By no means all his brother rabbis agreed with him. When Akiba, pointing at his leader cried, "There is the king, the Messiah!" Rabbi Johanan Ben Torta replied: "Akiba, the grass will be growing between your jawbones before the Son of David appears." Here again, it is easy to fall into an unbecoming self-righteousness, to say, "Politics and religion are two separate things, and should be kept separate". The origins of the Christian religion are interwoven with politics. It was politics that caused Jesus' parents to take him to Egypt as an infant; it was politics, above all, that caused Jesus' arrest and execution. The Passion, the climax of Jesus' earthly ministry, is from beginning to end a political drama.

As invariably happens, once extremism is in the field, moderation must hide its head. Bar Kokhba succeeded in occupying Jerusalem, and in restoring a makeshift Temple ritual, with Eleazar as high priest. He struck silver and bronze coins, the very symbol of independence. They bore representations of a temple, with a star above it, and in the background a Shrine of the Law, to stress the religious basis of the movement. The word *Jerusalem* appears on one side, and the words *Year I of the redemption of Israel* on the other. Later issues appeared in *Year II*. Yet other coins, typical of the shabby makeshift régime they served, are simply bronze issues of Vespasian, Domitian, Nerva, Trajan and Hadrian, hammered down and overprinted.

Nevertheless, despite its origin and character, the revolt enjoyed initial success, as such revolts generally do. There must have been in Palestine at least ten thousand troops, even if the two legions, the VIth and Xth, were under strength: if the legions, the two wings and the four cohorts were all present and up to strength, the total number of Roman effectives would have been fourteen thousand. Of these, only a detachment would have been stationed in Jerusalem: some would be in Galilee, others in the south, and no doubt a large number would be at their headquarters in the capital of the province, that is to say Caesarea, the great port between Jaffa and Carmel. The rebels first of all adopted guerrilla tactics, to which Palestine has always proved, down to our own day, admirably suited. It appears from a sentence in Dio that there had recently been an earthquake, which had no doubt disorganised public security. He says that "the tomb of Solomon had collapsed" (never to this day to be seen again) and that "wild animals were roaming the streets of the towns", which they only do when the towns are deserted. The rebels certainly exploited the situation, by taking to the hills and there constructing elaborate "hides", cave being linked to cave by passages, and holes bored in the rock to admit light and air. Tineius Rufus, the governor and commanding officer of the Xth, found himself forced to disperse his troops, to meet the attacks directed at him from all sides. The rebellion had been planned carefully. Jews had come from other lands to help and sustain the rebels. Palestinian Gentiles joined in, eager for loot. Arms had been obtained by an ingenious method. Jewish smiths obtained contracts for the supply of arms to the Roman army. They then turned in defective weapons, of which the Roman quartermasters refused to take delivery. The Jewish contractors were left with them on their hands, well content. With his communications disrupted and supply impossible, Rufus decided to withdraw his forces to the frontier districts. This meant the abandonment of Jerusalem, which, owing to the destruction of the fortifications after the war of 66-71, and the levelling operations which preceded the building of the new colony, was no longer defensible.

The Son of the Star was a rigid legalist. No uncircumcised males were to be allowed in the New Jerusalem, and those who had concealed their origin (see page 142) were compelled to undergo the rite a second time. This meant also risking the death penalty, owing to Hadrian's ban. More moderate Jews had already substituted for circumcision a ritual bath, borrowed from the Christians, as proselytes to Judaism could hardly be expected to risk a capital sentence at the very outset of their adherence. (See Babylonian Talmud, *Yebamoth* 46a and 71a). But no such common sense could sway Bar Kokhba. He also did something else, which was to prove a disaster to his nation. He persecuted the Christians. In his rôle of Messiah, he found particularly obnoxious those who not only refused to acknowledge his Messianic quality, but went further and worshipped One whom they knew to have been the only true Messiah. It is from this act that the final separation of Jews and Christians is to be dated (though some Jewish apologists would place the responsibility on the later Christian Councils). Between the year 70 and the year 132 there had been a period of polemic between Jews and Christians, without a complete break. But Bar Kokhba's execution of Christians caused the Christian attitude to harden into the tragic hostility which has ended only in our own day, when the Judaeo-Christian ethic has been assailed by a paganism more terrible than any of old, and the Jewish genius, in an unexampled flowering, has enriched the life of grateful Gentiles in so many different ways.

The course of the war—for such the revolt soon became—is hard to follow, because it is so scantily described by ancient writers. Fortunately, archaeology fills some of the gaps. Bar Kokhba's first task was to put Jerusalem into a state of defence. He knew that it could be attacked only on the north, the side from which Pompey and Titus had both in their turn assaulted it. He therefore ordered the construction of a rampart on the summit of the ridge about five hundred yards north of the present north wall, which stands on the foundations of the wall which Titus had destroyed. Of this rampart, considerable traces have come to light at various times during the last century. It ran from the hill on which the Russian buildings now stand, right down to the brow of the Kedron valley. It shews every sign of hasty construction. Great blocks dragged from the ruins of the north wall, small stones collected on the spot, paving flags, all were worked into this rebel rampart. It was provided with a gate at the point where the road to the north passes what is now the American School. "In short," says Abel, "this wall, the fourth of the series of walls which have successively enclosed the area of the city on the north, was in keeping with all the institutions of the precarious régime of Bar Kokhba. It produces on the imagination the same impression of poverty as the farthings and bronze coins overprinted by the rebels."

Tineius Rufus appealed to the governor of Syria for reinforcements. The governor, Publicius Marcellus, handing over the government of Syria to the commanding officer of the IVth, Scythian, hurried south to help. Meanwhile, Hadrian, realising how serious the situation was, decided to send his best general, and later to go to the field of battle himself. When Nero had been faced with the insurrection of 66, he sent to quell it a general who had done well in Britain. Hadrian now did the same. He recalled Sextus Julius Severus, who was then governing our island, and placed him in command in Palestine. The importance of the war is attested by the number of troops who were eventually engaged in it, which are known to us from the decorations bestowed on them, as recorded in inscriptions. Besides the VIth and Xth, and the IIIrd, Gallica, which Marcellus had brought with him, the IIIrd, Cyrenaican, with two cohorts of Arab levies, came over from Arabia. Egypt sent up the XXIInd, with a cohort of Damascenes. So pressing was the need, so grave the emergency, that legions were summoned from what are now Rumania, Austria, and Germany, even from beyond the Danube from Dacia, thus leaving the northern frontier dangerously bare. There were also contingents of Gauls, Thracians, Galatians and Palestinian Greeks. This large army was spread out all over the country, for Galilee had joined the rebellion; but it was in Judaea, Mount Royal as it was called, that the resistance was fiercest. Rabbi Akiba egged on the inhabitants by declaring that salvation would come only from Judah and Benjamin (the tribes to which the region had traditionally been assigned in the days of Joshua). The rebels inflicted heavy losses on the imperial troops. The XXIInd was wiped out, though this disaster was possibly due to poisoned wine sold to them by Jews.

Severus, like Vespasian before him, understood from his British experience that in a country of wild hills, where every rock and cave was known to the defenders, to make large-scale frontal attacks was to court disaster. He sent out numerous small detachments, to raid food supplies, and to cut communications, hoping to wear down the enemy without exposing his own troops. This strategy, he knew, would take time, but it was successful. Hadrian himself had returned to Palestine when he saw how dangerous the state of affairs had become. Once again, he consulted his old engineer-architect, Apollodorus, whom he asked to

Hadrian's Villa. The Island Pavilion (page 172).

Canopus looking towards the Serapeum.

Canopus seen from the Serapeum (page 172).

design a new kind of catapult, not for use against towns but against large concentrations of men who had occupied the hill-tops. Jerusalem was besieged, taken, and yet again destroyed. Hadrian reported the good news to the senate, but in view of the heavy casualties his army had suffered and the ignoble character of the war, he omitted the usual formula of a victorious general: "If you and your children are well, all is well: I and the armies are all in good health." Soon after the fall of Jerusalem, Hadrian returned to Rome, where he is known to have been on 5th May, 134. The fall of Jerusalem may therefore be placed early in the same year.

While this book was in preparation, documents came to light from the caves of Muraba'at, by the Dead Sea, which throw light on the war, and Bar Kokhba's part in it. One is a letter from him, telling a subordinate that he is not to mistreat certain Galilean refugees—which shews that Galilee was once again under Roman rule. Another shews us that Bar Kokhba had set up a sort of military capital of a makeshift government in the Herodium, the Palace-Tomb of Herod the Great near Bethlehem, with district offices at Engeddi and other places. Thus, after the fall of Jerusalem resistance still continued. Even when the Herodium fell, the war was not over. The stronghold of Bettir, which stands above the railway line a few miles south-west of Jerusalem, was chosen for the last stand of the Jews. Traces of the Roman wall of circumvallation still exist. In rabbinical literature, the defence became a saga, just as Bar Kokhba himself was to be exalted into the Last of the Heroes. In truth the final scenes must have been tragic. Bar Kokhba killed his own uncle, whom he suspected of wishing to surrender. Bettir fell in August 136, on the 9th Ab, the very same day as had witnessed the destruction of the Temple in the year 70. In Jewish eyes the two disasters were comparable, Bar Kokhba was killed. In Galilee Rufus hunted down the poor rabbis who had been seduced into supporting the revolt, and executed them, including Akiba who died under torture, stead-fastly testifying with his dying breath to the unity of God. Hadrian was hailed as *imperator* for the second time, and the senate and people voted him a monument to commemorate his triumph. On the emperor's proposal, Severus was voted the ornaments of a triumph, the last Roman commoner ever to receive them.

Bar Kokhba's fanaticism had ruined his country. Dio tells us that the Romans had destroyed fifty fortresses and 985 villages, and had killed more than half a million of the inhabitants, not counting those who had died by famine, fire or disease, so that the land had become a wilderness, where wolves and hyenas battened on the corpses. The last scene in this drama of futility was the saddest. Hundreds of captives were dragged down to Hebron, and there, on the site which their patriarch Abraham had hallowed, were sold like cattle. Four went for a measure of barley, but still there were not enough buyers, so the remainder were sent on to Gaza, where, in the very city that for them stood for uncleanness, Hadrian had recently built a temple and had instituted an annual fair. Here the remnants of the captives were sold.

Thus ended a war which had lasted for three and a half years. It brought disaster on Jewry, of which the effects were to last down to our own day. Bettir is still called, in the vernacular, the *Ruin of the Jews*. No site ever had a truer name. To round off the score, Hadrian also offended the Samaritans. On the summit of their holy mountain he erected a temple to Zeus, and embellished it with bronze doors taken from the Temple of Jerusalem. The newly founded pagan town of Neapolis, now Nablus, flourished, and became the resort of all the philosophic schools of the day. Its coins, in the succeeding reign, bore representations of the temple on Mount Gerizim, which was reached by a staircase of one thousand five hundred steps.

The new colony could now arise under the supervision of Aquila of Sinope in Pontus, later to become both Christian and Jew. Hadrian's Aelia is of great interest to us even today, for it was Hadrian who gave to the Holy City the layout which it has preserved in all essentials to our own time. Before his re-planning of the city, the main streets had run from the palace on the west, the modern citadel, down to the Temple. In this quarter were the markets and main government offices. The town had gradually spread to the north, and successive walls had been added on that side to protect the New City, as it was called. Hadrian quite altered these ancient "lines of force". The main street of his new colony, like that of all Roman colonies, should run north and south. So it was done; and to this day, as we walk through the Damascus Gate, and along the covered Suqs, out to the southern wall, it is along Hadrian's *Cardo maximus*, or chief way, that we walk. The Temple area was excluded from the new colony, which had no use for the relics of that despised and defeated cult. That is why the triple gate of triumph, which survives today in the *Ecce Homo* arch and the altar of the church of the Dames de Zion, is sited so far to the west (see Plate 18).

Fortunately, we know what Hadrian's colony looked like, from the Madeba map (see Plate 17). The plan is the same today. The great pillar inside the north gate, now the Damascus Gate, has gone, overthrown, most likely, by the Persians in the year 614. But the gate is still called the Gate of the Pillar in Arabic, so tough is tradition in that country.

Hadrian not only excluded the Temple area from his plan, he obliterated the Sepulchre of Christ with a temple of Venus. This had the opposite effect to what he had intended, for when, in the year 326, the pious empress Helena came to Jerusalem to reclaim and consecrate the sites associated with the ministry and Passion of Christ, she had only to order the removal of the temple to find the Sepulchre beneath it.

The name Aelia, though naturally the Christians reverted to the Biblical one, was still current when the Moslems captured the city in the seventh century, and early Moslem writers used it. The plan is still there. To have given its present aspect to the Holy City is, ironically, not the least achievement of the man who tried to eradicate the Jews and never understood the Christians.

Chapter XXII

BENEFITS FORGOT

HADRIAN had conquered in Europe and in the Levant, he had charmed Asia and Hellas; but Rome itself, the imperial capital, and the hearts of its people he had neither captivated nor touched. At the beginning of his reign, he had been spurned as an alien, as a provincial upstart. Now, at the end of it, despite all he had done for Rome, for its safety, honour and welfare, he was still unregarded. The senate, for all his outward deference to them, knew that he had, both by his legal reforms and by his provincial policy, circumvented and outwitted them. The Italian members of that body were now out-numbered by the "provincials" which gave them an additional cause for resentment against the ruler who had deliberately elevated the provinces at the expense of the "motherland", which had itself been divided up into four judicial tetrarchies (see page 76), as though it were some Asiatic appanage. Moreover, Hadrian, as he toured the empire, had not infrequently uncovered inefficiency and corruption on the part of Romans who held colonial appointments. He had punished them with a severity which had laid him open to criticism and resentment. They and their like were now his natural enemies. Nor had Hadrian conciliated the populace. He had given them a fine new city, purged of old abuses, enriched and embellished with magnificent buildings. He had built two new bridges, he had controlled the Tiber. He had given them cleaner, airier houses. The difference between the Rome of the Flavians, half a century before, and the model city which Hadrian bequeathed to the Antonines may be gauged by comparing Ostia with Pompeii. The narrow streets, the huddled dwellings, the windowless walls of so many of the humbler Pompeiian dwellings have been replaced in the Ostia of Hadrian by airy, wide-windowed houses, two and three storeys high, and many of them standing in gardens. The difference is exactly analogous to the difference between a row of back-to-back tenements of a century ago and the beautiful homes in the "new towns" of our own day. The Romans were no more grateful for these amenities than the modern English are: their appetite, like that of the English, had grown with overfeeding, and they took it all as their right.

Hadrian had his faults, too. Adept as he had shewn himself to be at conciliating the army by his military knowledge and bearing, he lacked the common touch. Two instances of his gaucherie when dealing with the Roman populace have come down to us. In republican days the Roman people had been proud of their popular assemblies which in one form or another, had been their legislature. Under the emperors, who had no relish for popular political assemblies of any kind, the rights of the old assemblies had been gradually extinguished. The last law to be passed by a *Comitia* had been enacted in the reign of Nerva. This meant that the one and only popular assembly was now the vast audience in the hippodrome, or in one of the great amphitheatres. Only here could the emperor, who presided, establish contact with his people. One day, when Hadrian was present in the theatre, the populace was cheering itself hoarse at the prowess of some popular gladiator. The emperor, instead of indulging them, turned to the herald, who always stood at his side, just as the trumpeter stands beside the *alguazils* in the bullring today, and said, "Tell them to shut up." The herald, saying to himself, "Does he think he is Domitian?" tactfully forbore to call the audience to order so peremptorily (and so ineffectually). Instead, he held up his hands, as though he had some important announcement to make. Gradually the hubbub subsided. When the crowd was silent and attentive, he simply said: "That is what the emperor wanted." Hadrian realised that the man had saved him from a gaffe and thanked him. On another occasion Hadrian was present at the horse-races in the hippodrome. The brilliance of a certain jockey had so delighted the crowd that they clamoured to the emperor for his liberation, for he was, like nearly all his profession, a slave. Hadrian had only to send for the man's owner, and either suggest that he free him, or offer to buy him and then free him himself. Either gesture would have charmed his subjects, at such little cost. Instead, Hadrian ordered one of his heralds to carry round the hippodrome (for no voice could be heard throughout the vast U) a placard on which was written: "You have no right to demand the freedom of a slave who is not your own property, nor to ask me to secure it for you." Could such a man be popular?

Finally, every Roman, and the Romans of that day as of this were intensely proud of being Roman, knew only too well that Hadrian had slighted their city, that he had rarely even lived in it, and that he made no secret of his preference for Athens and for all things Greek. It was too late now for Hadrian ever to come to terms with Rome: he had affronted the Romans too deeply and too long. To add to the sorrow of the emperor's homecoming, he knew that he was an ailing man. The first warning symptoms had been violent and prolonged attacks of nose-bleeding. He was suffering, this great athlete, who had tramped so many thousands of miles in all weathers, the penalty that not infrequently is exacted of such men—his arteries were hardening. This caused his blood-pressure to rise, his heart to become overstrained, dropsy to set in. By a curious chance, the last illness of Hadrian arose from the same causes, and ran the same course, as that of another great administrator, athlete and builder, Herod the Great. It was also to produce the same terrible consequences, in deterioration of character, savage vindictiveness and accesses of cruel rage.

Thus it happened that Rome and the Romans saw most of Hadrian when he had ceased to be himself. To this, and to the facts related above, is to be attributed the animosity with which his memory was assailed and his benefactions forgotten. His enemies were to declare not only that he was a man of two contrary characters, a Jekyll and Hyde case as we should say now, but even that his former benevolence had been no more than a mask for his natural viciousness.

But Hadrian was still Hadrian. He was still the prudent planner. He must think calmly about the future, and that he could not do as an alien in an alien capital. Eight years before, in 126, Hadrian had started to build himself a villa at Tibur, a lovely village some fifteen miles to the east of Rome, in the skirts of the Sabine hills. He was by no means the first to choose this smiling locality. Even in republican days, many a rich Roman had made Tibur his country retreat. Scipio, Marius, Maecenas—they all had delighted in Tibur, in the falls of the river Anio, which were in later ages to provide the Villa D'Este with its fantastic cascades and Rome with its first electric illumination. Horace the poet preferred Tibur to all other resorts, and had a country-house in its neighbourhood. Hadrian had selected his site not, like some of his predecessors and successors, for the summer but for the winter. That is to say, instead of siting his villa on one of the loftier terraces of the hills, he chose the plain below, a locality which the peasants still call the *Costacalda* the "hot side". After his experience of England and Germany, Hadrian wanted, like so many English and Germans, at all costs to be warm in winter. In the summer he could always go, like the Romans of a later age, *"ad aquas"*, to the seaside.

"Villa" is a misnomer for the estate which Hadrian laid out. He designed his creation to be not merely a sumptous imperial dwelling-place: there were already plenty of those. There was a pavilion at Baiae on the Bay of Naples, there was the villa of Livia, Augustus' consort, north of Rome, famous for its frescoes, there was Hadrian's own charming little hunting-box at Praeneste, which set the precedent for Tibur by abandoning the old Etruscan hill-town for the level tilth it overlooks. What Hadrian desired to create at Tibur was something far more startling, in fact un-precedented. He planned what we should now call an Empire Exhibition (albeit an eclectic one), a whole Garden City to recreate in miniature the regions of the empire which had most caught the fancy of their imperial inspector. Besides the palace, therefore, with its essential annexes such as barracks, baths and theatres, there were to be reproductions of famous buildings in Athens—the Lyceum, the Painted Porch, the Academy, the Town Hall. There was to be a grove to recall the Vale of Tempe in Thessaly and a subterranean Hades. Finally, and most signific-antly, there was to be a Canopus, the ancient port of the Nile Delta. Only the august and mysterious Egypt was to be allowed to share the honours with his beloved Hellas.

The area of this colossal fantasy, this dream in three dimensions, was no less than three-quarters the size of Rome itself, that is seven hundred and fifty acres as against one thousand, or more than twice the size of Roman London. Today only a quarter or less of the original remains; yet even this scanty relic constitutes one of the most impressive monuments of imperial Rome. Every section of it bears the stamp of Hadrian's genius. Groves of olives and cypress, of oak and bay with, in spring, fields of green corn below, fragrant with roses, and loud with the song of nightingales —these are the setting for rugged masses of russet and glaucous brick, standing like cliffs which have defied the onslaughts of time and nature. Domes and apses, colonnades, vast substructures, terraces, every variation that can suggest itself on the theme of architectural stability and grace, all are to be found in these forsaken vaults and ruined palaces. There was even a little round temple of Venus, with a circular colonnade of sixteen pure Doric columns, and a copy of Praxiteles' Aphrodite of Cnidus inside. There are two sections of the villa which impress the visitor with a particular intimacy, by their freshness and in- genuity, both having recently been restored by the Italian government under the skilled direction of Dr. Vighi. They are the Island Pavilion and the Canopus. The former (see Plate 25) is a masterpiece of the sheer aesthetic pleasure that a subtle use of columniation can give, the result being almost epicyclic, curve blending into curve, and plane into plane. It has all the grace of Greece, all the dignity of Rome. It is a masterpiece of its age, and wholly Hadrianic. To return to Rome and to contemplate the lifeless imitations which followed it is to appreciate once again the soaring, vital originality of Hadrian.

The Canopus impresses by its implications. Here, in Italy, the novel use of Italian idiom (see Plate 26) recreated a feeling of Egyptian mythological awe. The great cavern beneath the crag at the southern end of the canal, the Serapeum, even the statue of the crocodile, laughable as it may seem, all contribute to the feeling that solid immobile architecture can transport its beholder to the Delta itself. This section of the villa must have held for Hadrian a poignant significance, for with the god Serapis was associated the lost Antinoüs, who had passed to immortality beneath the waves of Serapis' own Nile. To this day the canal and the cavern seem holy and enchanted, and, even at noonday, despite the English swans that glide on the peaceful water, to be possessed by some unforgetting ghost. The recent excavations have yielded some magnificent statuary, caryatids, figures of the Tiber and the Nile, of a Silenus, an Ares and a Hermes, copies of those made by Myron in the fifth century B.C., and the best known copy of the Amazon of Phidias. Hadrian had personally ordered each one, and his taste is vindicated by their beauty. These treasures are still there for the pilgrim to behold; but for centuries Hadrian's villa was the richest mine in Italy for the recovery of heads and statues. Every collection of note in Europe, public and private, has one or more examples from the

A mosaic from Hadrian's Villa, now in the Vatican Museum. It shews a self-consciously "rural" scene.

The apotheosis of Sabina, now in the Museo dei Conservatori in Rome.

villa. One of the most successful dowsers for these treasures, and also the most honest, was the Briton, Gavin Hamilton, whose clientèle was the English nobility. He recovered many from Tibur; but his flair also led him to treasure-trove elsewhere. From the little villa at Praeneste, he brought back one of the finest heads of Antinoüs yet found, and in 1769, by dragging a lake, Pantanello, he secured, in one operation, no less than sixty marbles which had been preserved in the slime.

Chapter XXIII

"AND AFTER THAT, THE DARK"

SUCH was the sumptuous retreat in which Hadrian had planned to spend his latter years, home at last from his wanderings, surrounded yet by splendid souvenirs of the distant scenes he had loved. It was to have been the supreme harmony of town and country, of Rome and Hellas, in which the philosopher king would rule and dream. The reality was very different: a haggard wreck, only rarely able to leave his sick-bed, a forlorn mockery, in mind and body, now parodied the genial father of his country. But still he toiled on at the business of empire. How astute he could still be is shewn in a rescript—preserved for us on papyrus—which he sent in the year 136 to Egypt. The Nile, ironically enough, had once again been the cause of affliction, this time not to Hadrian but to the Egyptians themselves. They had complained to the emperor that the river had failed to rise two years in succession, and that they were being ruined. Hadrian, from his personal knowledge, could grasp the seriousness of the failure, and the necessity of relieving it. Hadrian also knew that any precedent he might set would be eagerly filed for future exploitation, and that while it was true that the Nile sometimes produced but scanty crops, it was equally true that in other years it produced crops of exceptional abundance and had recently done so. This is what he wrote:

"Having been informed that now, as last year, the Nile has been inadequate in its rise . . . although during a succession of previous years its rise was not only plentiful but almost higher than any year before, and flooding all over the country caused the production of abundant and flourishing crops—still I have deemed it necessary to bestow some relief upon the cultivators, although I hope, God willing, that in years to come any possible deficiencies will be supplied by the Nile itself, and the earth, according to the revolving nature of things, will change from prosperous flow and abundance to scarcity and from scarcity to plenty." Could any modern secretary of state produce a better reply?

Hadrian's mind, as the above document shews, was still alert, but as his disease gained upon him he knew that he must prepare for his own end, and the perpetuation of his work by others. Who was to succeed him?

In this last great crisis of his career, Hadrian was as baffling, as paradoxical, as at any earlier time.

Hadrian had no legitimate issue. His nearest blood relation was a boy of eighteen, called Fuscus, the grandson of his brother-in-law Servianus (see page 28), who was now ninety-one.

All Rome was talking, guessing, and whispering. One night at dinner Hadrian asked his guests to name ten men "worthy to be emperor". There was an awkward silence. "Well, nine, then," said Hadrian, "there's always Servianus." This remark went the rounds in no time. Whether it really did cause the old man and his grandson to think up some crazy plot we cannot be sure. What is certain is that they were both put to death. It was said that Servianus, when he received the fatal mandate, sent for a brazier, and throwing incense upon it called down upon Hadrian the terrible curse that when he longed for death, he should not be able to die.

The senate feared a new reign of terror. The death of the four consulars nearly twenty years before (see page 49) was recalled. Malicious rumours told of secret killings, forced suicides, banishments, confiscations. That Hadrian in his growing derangement and agony did order executions is certain, because we are expressly told that some of the intended victims were saved by the intervention of Antoninus.

Whomsoever Hadrian chose as his heir, he was bound to offend the disgruntled and frightened senate. Nevertheless, his first choice must cause astonishment. He hit on a handsome young fop called Lucius Ceionius Commodus, scion of an ancient Etruscan family, many of whom had risen to the consulate, his father having held the office just thirty years before. He had married the daughter of Nigrinus, the former conspirator, and in the year of his adoption their little boy also called Lucius was six. On his adoption Lucius Ceionius Commodus added the name of Hadrian's family, Aelius, to his own, and was also granted the title Caesar. He was henceforth known as Lucius Aelius (Verus) Caesar. This last name, originally born by the great Julius, had become one of the "royal titles"; it was henceforth to be that of the heir to the throne only, like our Prince of Wales, and like that title was an honorific, not an office, and did not imply any authority to share in the government. The grant of the title, on these terms, to Lucius marks an important step in the transformation of the Roman principate into a hereditary monarchy.

Lucius was a man of "royal beauty", a dilettante and an amorist. He was very fond of flowers. He had a bed made of four great cushions, covered with a gauze net filled with rose-petals, beneath a coverlet of lilies. Anointed with the finest Persian scent, he liked to lie and read Martial's epigrams—"my Virgil", he called them—or Ovid's *Book of Love*, or a fashionable cookery-book. He invented a special dish for his new father, made of pheasant, peacock, ham in batter, wild boar and sow's udders. He called his pages after the winds, and tied wings on them to make them look like cupids. When his wife complained of his affairs with other women, he blandly replied: "Don't interfere: I have a good time with them: 'wife' is a term of honour, not of enjoyment."

Such was the man whom Hadrian had chosen to be heir to the Roman Empire. On what grounds had he made his choice? Naturally, there were plenty of people who said that Lucius had been chosen for his looks; but clearly Hadrian must have had some other firmer grounds. Many good scholars, including Carcopino, have concluded that Lucius was, in fact, a natural son of Hadrian. There is no direct evidence of this but the inference is very strong. To celebrate his adoption, Hadrian distributed a largesse of no less than three million pounds, most of which went to his faithful army. Lucius was made consul (he had been praetor six years before) and was sent off to govern Pannonia, on the Danube frontier. In a few months, he was back again, dying of consumption. He lived through the year 137, and was to have delivered a New Year's Day address to Hadrian, on 1st January, 138. The speech, "a very beautiful one", was composed and was afterwards published, but Lucius never delivered it. On that same New Year's Day he died in his sleep, of a haemorrhage.

During the young man's illness, Hadrian had been beside himself with grief. Sometimes he had been bitter: "We have wasted three million! We have leaned against a tottering wall, which can hardly bear my weight, far less that of the empire." The officious prefect who repeated this remark to Lucius, thus making him

Succession. The first choice, Lucius Aelius Caesar
(Table III).

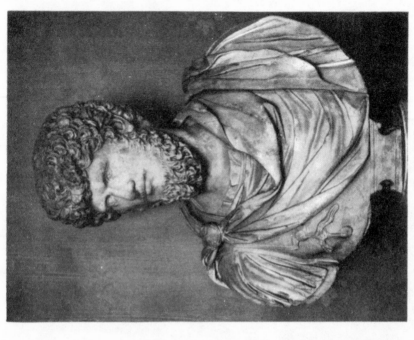

The eventual successors: Marcus Aurelius (*left*) and Lucius Verus (Table III).

worse, was deprived of his office. Sometimes Hadrian would shew a wry fortitude: "I seem to have adopted not a son, but a god"—alluding to the practice of deifying dead members of the imperial house. Sometimes he was gentle. He would walk up and down in the groves of Tibur, reciting the famous and pathetic lines in which Virgil commemorated Marcellus, the nephew and heir-presumptive of Augustus, lines so poignant that when Virgil first read them, the boy's mother fainted with emotion. One of his friends, hearing him repeat:

> "*Ostendent terris hunc tantum fata neque ultra*
> *Esse sinent*"
> "This hero Fate will but display to earth
> Nor suffer him to stay."

continued the quotation:

> "*nimium vobis Romana propago*
> *Visa potens, superi, propria haec si dona fuissent*"
> "The race of Rome
> Would seem to you, O Gods, to be too great
> Were such gifts to endure."

Whereupon Hadrian said to him: "Those lines do not apply to Verus' life," and added:

> "*Manibus date lilia plenis;*
> *Purpureos spargam flores animamque nepotis*
> *His saltem accumulem donis et fungar inani*
> *Munere.*"
> "Bring lilies with a bounteous hand;
> And I the while will scatter rosy blooms,
> Thus doing honour to our kinsman's soul
> With these poor gifts—though useless be the task."

To anyone acquainted with the original, as Hadrian's friends were, these lines spoken in that context could have been spoken only by a father mourning a son. We are in fact expressly told by the chronicler that Hadrian did mourn for Verus as a father, rather than as an emperor. He was buried in the family mausoleum, statues of him were raised throughout the empire, temples were built. Most significant of all, when Hadrian chose his next heir, he gave Lucius' son, the little Lucius, whom he had kept on in the palace, to be adopted by Antoninus "as if he were his own grandson"; and he often remarked: "Let the empire keep something of Verus." It is not to be supposed that Hadrian would have acted in this manner, maintaining for a second generation the imperial connection which the first had hardly seemed to warrant, unless beneath mere sentiment there had lain the deeper bond of blood.

A new heir must now be found. Hadrian told his council that "as he had no child of his own"—which was certainly true now—he must select one, and that a chosen heir was better than a natural one, because it was easier to find virtue than to transmit it. He had chosen, he said, Titus Aurelius Fulvus Boionius Arrius Antoninus, in fact he had chosen him even before Aelius died. He formally recommended him to the senate on his birthday, the last he was to see, the 24th January, A.D. 138, and a month later, on the 25th February, adopted him as his son. Antoninus was a man of fifty-one, of excellent antecedents, his father's family having come from Nîmes, and his mother's having adorned public life for several generations. Antoninus was handsome, talented, kind and calm. He was a just landlord, and a thrifty administrator. In fact he was a Roman of the old school, which had seemed almost extinct. He had been one of the four Italian commissioners (see page 76), and had governed Asia (see page 104). He was an old friend of Hadrian, with whom he had great influence. Now that the emperor was free to choose on the grounds of merit only, he made the best possible choice.

But Hadrian was looking farther ahead than one life. He wanted to ensure that the empire should be in wise hands for as long as possible, that his own great work should not perish. He therefore made it a condition of Antoninus' adoption that he in his turn should adopt both the younger Aelius and also Marcus Annius Verus, then a boy of sixteen, a nephew of Antoninus. Here again Hadrian's choice was impeccable. The little Marcus Annius Verus was to become the emperor and philosopher Marcus Aurelius. Before that he was to become not only Antoninus' nephew and adopted son, but his son-in-law, by marrying his daughter Annia. Thus the Antonines, as the family came to be called, were united not merely by reasons of state but by personal alliances (see Table III).

The settling of this succession, which was to make the phrase "the Antonine Age" a synonym for unparalleled felicity and peace, was Hadrian's last achievement and one of his greatest. But he had another six months to linger. He was all alone now. Antinoüs was dead, Lucius was dead, Sabina, who had never loved him but had never left him, she, too, had died in the year 137. The emperor, also, now wished only to die. Voluntary suicide was a crime, he knew. But he had allowed the aged philosopher Euphrates to commit suicide on compassionate grounds. Could he not claim a like indulgence? He even ordered a servant, a wild captive from the north who had been his huntsman, to stab him, shewing him the exact spot on his breast at which he was to aim the knife. The slave hurried off to tell Antoninus, who with the prefects came to Hadrian to implore him to face death with resignation. He himself, he said, would be nothing but a parricide if he allowed Hadrian to be killed. The court swarmed with mountebanks, astrologers and soothsayers. Hadrian "as it were, died daily". He begged his doctor to give him some poison, whereat the doctor took his own life rather than administer it. On another occasion servants snatched the dagger from Hadrian's own hand.

The Roman summer, the last of Hadrian's life, was at hand, and even the great vaults of the villa were no sure bulwark against the still and stifling heat. Hadrian, summoning his dying spirits to a final effort, set out on his last journey, to Baiae, the beautiful thermal resort on the horned northern tip of the Bay of Naples, which seems to be of Italy but not in it; for from its terraces, in the solitude of the little peninsula, far from the noise and bustle of the harbours and highways, the panorama of that most lovely gulf unfolds itself, Capri, Naples, Vesuvius, Pozzuoli. Behind the imperial villa lay the mysterious grottoes, the abode of the inspired Sybil sung by Virgil, whose own tomb stood on the opposite shore, just north of Naples. In no more apt or more poetic setting could a Roman emperor take his leave of life. This Hadrian did in lines which have ever since been famous:

> "Animula, blandula, vagula,
> Hospes comesque corporis
> Quae nunc abibis in loca,
> Pallidula, rigida, nudula?
> Nec ut soles dabis jocos?"

"Warming, wand'ring little sprite
Body's guest and company,
Whither now take you your flight,
Cold and comfortless and white,
Leaving all your jollity?"

Hadrian had lived sixty-two years, five months and seventeen days. He had been emperor of Rome for twenty years and eleven months.

Antoninus, in whose arms Hadrian had expired, assisted by Hadrian's secretary Celer, carried the body back round the bay to Pozzuoli, where it was given a makeshift resting-place, in the grounds of what had once been Cicero's villa. The senate wished to annul Hadrian's acts, and to refuse him deification. But Antoninus, whose agnomen *Pius* derives from his devotion to his defunct adoptive father, pointed out that to annul Hadrian's acts would be to annul his own adoption, and even persuaded the senate to ratify Hadrian's deification. Finally, Hadrian was laid to rest in his own great monument by the Tiber. Antoninus built a temple for him at Pozzuoli, where he had been temporarily buried until the Roman tomb was completed, established a quinquennial contest in his honour and appointed priests and fraternities to venerate his memory. In Rome itself a splendid temple was raised to his name, in which the provinces he had served so well were represented by symbolic figures. Part of the fabric of this temple is now incorporated in the Rome Bourse. Thus, at long last, the emperor whom in life Rome had rejected was in death received and revered by Rome.

Epilogue

PHANTOM AND FACT

THE antique world interests mankind only as it prefigures, reflects, or contrasts with our own day: there is small profit in an antiquarianism which merely seeks to revive "what mankind has conspired to forget". In this respect Hadrian must still command our attention. The man himself may remain a shadow, but his work is with us today. It consists of three main achievements, the first two willed, the third involuntary.

To start with, it was Hadrian who by his legal administrative and military reforms made possible the Antonine age, that is the reigns of Antoninus Pius and Marcus Aurelius, which with that of Hadrian cover the years A.D. 117 to 180. These six decades were the most splendid and tranquil epoch of the Roman Empire, and they were the achievement of Hadrian. In his lifetime Hadrian preferred that his works, even his memoirs, should bear the names of others; his greatest political memorial similarly bears the name of the man whom Hadrian chose to maintain it. The Roman Empire has passed away from the earth, but not from the minds of men, nor is it likely ever to do so. To have fashioned its greatest era, the apogee of its authority, is alone claim enough upon the veneration and gratitude of mankind.

Hadrian's second bequest to our world is his architecture. No one artist has ever left so deep an imprint over so wide an area. The Athens of Pericles, the London of Wren—many another city has been the creation of a single mind. But Hadrian left the mark of his genius not only upon Rome, but upon Athens, Trebizond, Jerusalem, Cyrene and Newcastle, upon Asia, Africa, Europe and England. Apart from the poignancy which such relics must always possess, the surviving remnants of Hadrian's architecture have a vitality, beauty and rhythm which are of germinal importance to the town-planners and builders of our own age.

But the irony of Hadrian's legacy to us lies in his third achievement—the religious development which he never intended, but made inevitable. That this sensitive artist had a cold, an almost repulsive side, has already, perhaps, been made clear. There were certain classes of men whom he could not win, or never sought to win. This human insensitiveness is not infrequently the price of artistic sensibility. In Hadrian's case it was shewn in his dealings with the Jews. The nationalism of the Jewish extremists, the ruthless selfishness of the patriotic scoundrels, was quite incompatible with Roman, or any other, rule. But the Jews had for many generations shewn that they could, if they were wisely and humanely treated, be among the most trustworthy, industrious and morally elevated citizens of the empire. After the suppression of the revolt of A.D. 66-70, the Jews had been harshly punished. But gradually the harshness had been softened, and a more tolerant attitude had replaced it. Nevertheless, Jewish resentment still smouldered, Roman rigour still exacerbated it with what dire results has been related in this narrative. Hadrian's action after the war profoundly changed the whole direction of Jewish history, and so of Christian history as well, because, whatever its later conquests in its own right, in its origin the Christian faith was Jewish, in the words of its Founder to the woman of Samaria: "Ye worship that which ye know not; we worship that which we know: for salvation is from the Jews." By Hadrian's day, as indeed, from the days of the apostles, the Christian faith had won many gentile hearts; it was no longer a Jewish "way", although many pagans might treat it as though it were. Nevertheless, until the time of Bar Kokhba, there had been no irrevocable break between Jew and Christian. Bar Kokhba precipitated it, but it was Hadrian who made it irrevocable, by banishing the Jews from Jerusalem and replacing the city itself with a pagan creation peopled by imported Gentiles. Hadrian ensured that the Mother Church of Christianity should cease to be Jewish, which up to that time it had predominantly been. Rome had not yet acquired the primacy that she was later, as the see of St. Peter, to win, Constantinople had yet to be founded. The position of the Mother Church of Jerusalem, the cradle of the faith, the guardian of the holy sites which even then were the magnet of the pilgrim's heart, was therefore of the first importance in the mind of every Christian. So long as that Church had been composed of men of Jewish race, and under the direction of a Jewish bishop, the link between the old and the new dispensations remained strong and bright. Now, it was broken.

Hadrian did not realise what he had done, because he was not interested in Christianity and he detested Judaism. He was anaesthetised with his synthetic Hellenism. Nevertheless, it was Hadrian who, by sundering Christianity from its Jewish matrix, ensured that it should become more and more the faith of his own Gentiles. In this way he was the unwitting forerunner of Constantine, and of the triumph of the faith in his own Rome. Is it not ironical that the pilgrim in Jerusalem, as he walks the last few furlongs that lead him to the Sepulchre of his Lord, is treading the very street which was the main thoroughfare of Hadrian's Aelia, that the pilgrim in Rome, to reach the basilica of St. Peter in the Vatican, crosses the Tiber on the very bridge which Hadrian built to give access to his own memorial?

Of such strange webs is history woven. The interest of Hadrian to the contemporary world is that of a man who tried to see the problems of his age, political, social and spiritual, as a single problem, and to find a solution for it. He was, in part, successful, he bequeathed to later ages a magnificent treasure of achievement. But in the realm of the spirit he failed, and it is the spiritual failures who are, always, the most tragic, and the most to be loved.

Table I

THE ROMAN EMPERORS,
27 B.C.–A.D. 222

B.C.

27 Augustus

A.D.

14 Tiberius
37 Caius (Caligula)
41 Claudius
54 Nero
68, ⎰ Galba
69 ⎱ Otho
      Vitellius
69 Vespasian
79 Titus
81 Domitian

96   Nerva
98   Trajan
117 Hadrian
138 Antoninus Pius
161 Marcus Aurelius
180 Commodus
      ⎰ Pertinax
193 ⎰ Didius Julianus
      ⎱ Septimius Severus
211 Caracalla
217 Macrinus
218 Elagabalus
222 Alexander Severus

Table II

HADRIAN AND HIS ANCESTORS

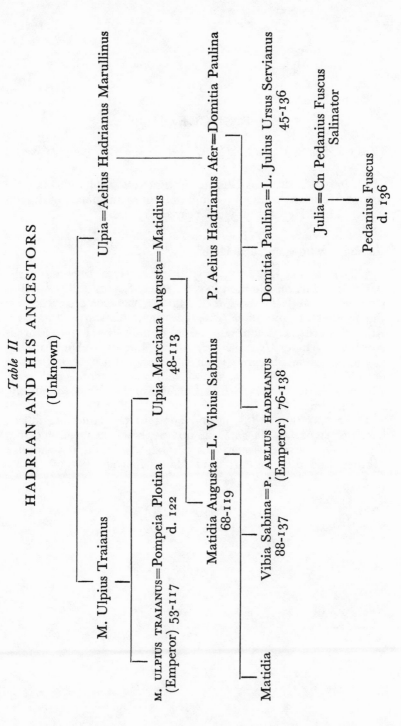

(Unknown)

Ulpia=Aelius Hadrianus Marullinus

M. Ulpius Traianus

M. ULPIUS TRAIANUS=Pompeia Plotina
(Emperor) 53-117   d. 122

Ulpia Marciana Augusta=Matidius
48-113

P. Aelius Hadrianus Afer=Domitia Paulina

Matidia Augusta=L. Vibius Sabinus
68-119

Matidia

Vibia Sabina=P. AELIUS HADRIANUS
88-137   (Emperor) 76-138

Domitia Paulina=L. Julius Ursus Servianus
45-136

Julia=Cn Pedanius Fuscus
Salinator

Pedanius Fuscus
d. 136

Table III

THE SUCCESSION

(The names in italics are those by which their bearers are generally known)

1. *First Choice:* Lucius Ceionius Commodus (probably a natural son of Hadrian) who, on adoption, took the name of Lucius *Aelius Caesar*. He died on New Year's Day, 138.

2. *Second Choice:* Titus Aurelius Fuluius Boionius Arrius *Antoninus*, who succeeded Hadrian as emperor.

3. *To be eventual joint successors of Antoninus*, Hadrian chose (*a*) the son of (1), who, on adoption took the name Lucius Aelius Aurelius Commodus, and (*b*) the son of Marcus Annius Verus who was the brother of Antoninus' wife Faustina, this son was also M. Annius Verus, and on adoption he took the name Marcus Aurelius. When *Marcus Aurelius* and Lucius Aelius Aurelius Commodus (3*a*) became joint emperors, *Marcus Aurelius* gave both his daughter, Lucilla, and his family name, to his colleague, who was thenceforth known as Lucius Annius Verus, or, simply, as *Lucius Verus*.

There was thus a "dynastic" bond in the Antonine fabric, because (*i*) *Marcus Aurelius* was first nephew, then adopted son, then son-in-law to *Antoninus*, and (ii) *Lucius Verus* was first adoptive brother, and then son-in-law to *Marcus Aurelius*.

INDEX

Ben Torta, Rabbi Johanan, 161
Berenice (Benghazi), 152, 153
Berenson, Bernard, 60
Berytus, see Beirut
Bettir ("Ruin of the Jews"), 165, 166
Bithynia, 42, 55, 96, 97, 98, 99, 143
   Bithynian, 100, 155, 156
Boadicea, 83, 84
Bona Dea, temple of, 115
Book of Love, Ovid's, 176
Borysthenes (Hadrian's horse), 92
Bostra, 134
Brigantes, the, 83, 84
Britain
   cultural complexions of, 82, 86
   cities in, development of, 85-6, 89, 181
   Hadrian in, 85-90, 181
   Roman occupation of, 43, 74, 81-90
   Roman relics in, 82
British Empire, differences from Roman,
   132-3
British Museum, 100
Buckingham, James Silk, 159
Burke, Edmund, 57
Byblos, 131

Caesar, Julius, 17, 33, 48, 82, 119, 127,
   138, 149, 153, 175
Caesars, Julian the Apostate's, 155
Caligula, Emperor, 18, 53, 83, 102
Cambridge Ancient History, 69
Cambyses, King, 158
Camden, 89
Campus Martius, 116
Capitol, Rome, 20, 55
Capitolinus, Jupiter, see Jupiter
Cappadocia, 98, 127, 128, 133
Caracalla, 158
Caractacus, 83
Carcopino, Jérôme, 64, 176
Cardinals, College of, 31-2, 70
Caria, 126
Carthage, 118-22, 137
   Hadrianopolis, 120
   Rome, 127
   wars with, 119, 120
   Zama, 120
Casius, Mount, 129
Cassius, Dio, 29, 84
Castel Sant' Angelo, Rome, 116
Catiline conspiracy, 54
Cato, 61, 120
Catullinus, 121, 122
Celer, 180
Celsus, Publilius, 48, 49
Cephisus, 124
Chadanne, Georges, 109
Chosroes, King, 128
Christians, the, 64, 65, 147
   Christian Councils, 163
   Christian history, Hadrian's effect on,
      15, 182-3
   Jews, relations with, 136, 143, 160, 161
   Rome, persecutions by, 140-5, 167

Chrysostom, Dion, 55, 56, 157
Cicero, 22, 54, 61, 102, 107, 120, 180
Cilicia, 126
Clark, Sir Kenneth, 100
Clarus, Septicius, 51
Claudiopolis, 99
Claudius, Emperor, 18, 71, 74
   Britain, in, 83, 84, 98, 138
Clement, bishop of Rome, 142
Cleopatra, 17, 94, 119, 153
Colchester, 83, 84
   Claudian temple at, 84
Cologne, 35
Colosseum, Rome, 20, 21, 24, 109, 112
Commagene, 127, 133
Commodus, Lucius Ceionius, 175-9
Constantine the Great, 70, 183
Corinth, 101, 107
Corpus Papyrorum Judaicorum, 138
Cossutius, 125
Ctesiphon, 42
Cumont, Franz, 65
Cybele, 64, 65
Cyprus, 43, 80, 124, 131, 139
Cyrene, 37, 43, 139, 151, 152, 159, 181
   Hadrian relics in, 153
Cyzicus, 97

Dacia, 37-40, 42, 48, 53, 74, 81
Damascus, 131, 134
   museum of, 130
Daphne, park of, 126
Dawkins, Professor, 62
Decapolis, 133, 134
Decebalus, King, 38-9
Deir al-Qala, 131
Delphi, 107
Demosthenes, 37
Description of the East, 158
Dialogues, the, 103
Dido, 119
Dionysius of Miletus, 104
Dionysus, 102, 156
   theatre of, 101, 124
Domitian, Emperor, 18, 19, 27, 28, 29,
   30, 31, 32, 33, 38, 41, 48, 53, 55,
   68, 72, 85, 139, 143, 169
Domitian, Suetonius's, 139
d'Orgeval, Bernard, 78, 144
Druids, the, 83

Egypt, 41, 43, 67, 80, 91, 131
   deities of, 64
   Roman granary, 153-4
Eleazar, Rabbi, 147
Eleusis, 123, 156
Emerita (Merida), 22, 25
Ennius, 61
Epameinondas, 107, 149
Ephesus, 80, 95, 96, 100, 104, 126
Epictetus, 103
Epicureans, the, 63
Epiphanes, Antiochus, 103, 125, 137,
   148, 149

189